十三仏

The 13 Buddhas
Tracing the Roots of the Thirteen Buddha Rites

Steven.J.Hutchins

www.13buddhas.com

Copyright © 2015 Steven.J.Hutchins

All rights reserved.

ISBN-10: 1511579595
ISBN-13: 978-1511579599

DEDICATION

To the memory of Arthur.H.Hutchins

CONTENTS

The Main Japanese Buddhist Sects — 1
Introduction — 9
Introducing the Thirteen Buddhas — 15

PART ONE: THE THIRTEEN BUDDHA RITES IN SCRIPTURE

1. Seven Seventh-day Rites — 44
2. The Scripture on the Ten Kings — 50
3. The Scripture on Jizō and the Ten Kings — 54
4. Kōbō Daishi Gyakushu Nikkinokoto — 58
5. Esoteric Interpretations — 64

PART TWO: ARCHAEOLOGICAL EVIDENCE OF THIRTEEN BUDDHA RITES

6. Hotsuki Rokumensekidō — 74
7. Enmeiji Jyūnison Shuji Mandala — 78
8. Jikōji Jyūsanbutsu Shuji Itabi — 82
9. Haguro Jyūsanbutsu Dō Itabi — 86
10. Fukatani Jyūsanbutsu Gun — 88

Conclusion — 94

EPILOGUE

Thirteen Buddha Pilgrimage in Yamagata — 98
Glossary of Terms — 114
Bibliography — 117

ACKNOWLEDGMENTS

This book is an extension of my 2013 thesis submitted for a Masters of Arts at SOAS University of London. I'd like to thank Benedetta Lomi and Lucia Dolce for supporting and encouraging my research.
I would also like to extend my warmest gratitude to Komine Kazuko for kindly allowing me to use her wonderful illustrations of the Thirteen Buddhas in this book. Finally, thanks to hutchinscreative.co.uk for designing the front cover.

Key Historical Periods

Nara Period	710-794
Heian Period	794-1185
Kamakura Period	1185-1333
Muromachi Period	1333-1568
Momoyama Period	1568-1600
Edo Period	1600-1868

宗派の特徴
THE MAIN JAPANESE BUDDHIST SECTS

Buddhist art and literature arrived in Japan in the mid-sixth century from India via Korea and China. Initially, six great Chinese schools, known as the Six Sects of Nanto, were established around the ancient capitals of Asura and Nara. Gradually more schools developed, favoring their own particular Buddhist sutras and deities, and in the post-Meiji period, pre-WWII, thirteen schools of traditional Buddhism were officially recognized. For the reader unfamiliar with the main Japanese Buddhist sects, I shall provide a brief summary of them in the following pages.

ESOTERIC BUDDHISM (*mikkyō* 密教)

Esoteric Buddhism, also known as Vajrayāna or Tantric Buddhism, was introduced to Japan in the early ninth century. It stresses the importance of the three mysteries: meditation, mudra and mantra. Special focus is also placed on the transcendent power of symbols and signs to lead the practitioner to enlightenment. Mandalas play a central role as aids in eidetic meditation practices, and symbolic means of communicating higher truths deemed inexpressible through words.

Goma fire ceremonies are also a distinguishing characteristic, and they are carried out by priests to avert misfortunes, facilitate divine providence and subdue baleful influences. Esoteric Buddhist priests earned much favor with the ruling nobility in the Heian era as they were seen to hold genuine shamanic powers capable of protecting the imperial family and the welfare of the nation.

The overarching philosophy of Esoteric Buddhism is a radical non-dualism where the adept can come to realize the unity of self with the Buddha through the act of ritual practice. Disciples are taught that the totality of the elements form the body of the Buddha, and these very same elements form the body of every living being and object. Thus, in Esoteric Buddhism, one does not consider oneself as separated from the cosmos and nature.

SHINGON (真言宗)

The Shingon lineage of Esoteric Buddhism was founded by the eminent monk Kūkai, posthumously known as Kōbō Daishi (the great teacher). He was initiated into the esoteric Buddhist tradition by his master Hui-kuo in China, and returned to Japan to set up the Shingon Buddhist monastery in Mount Koya. "Shingon", meaning true word, is a Japanese rendition of the Sanskrit word for "mantra".

In Shingon Buddhist doctrine, Kūkai incorporated secret rites of Indian origin that he had learned in China, some of which were only to be transmitted orally from master to pupil. However, in the first half of the twentieth century, the texts of ritual manuals from certain Shingon schools became available to nonqualified practitioners for the first time. Consequently, a host of prominent Shingon rituals and meditation practices including visualizations on the moon (*gachirinkan* 月輪観), the planet venus (*gumonjihō* 求聞持法) and the Sanskrit seed syllable "A" (*ajikan* 阿字観) are now public knowledge (see Yamasaki, 1988). In Shingon, "A" is the seed syllable form of the cosmological Buddha Dainichi Nyorai. It stands for the original unborn nature of the universe, the root source of all things.

The motto sokushin jōbutsu 即身成仏, "to attain enlightenment in this very existence", became synonymous with Kūkai's Buddhism. Unlike other Buddhist sects, which maintained that enlightenment was only possible after numerous reincarnations, Kūkai asserted that it was possible to reach enlightenment now, without waiting for rebirth in another world.

TENDAI (天台宗)

The Tendai sect descends from the Chinese Tiantai school which based its teachings around the Lotus Sutra. The Tendai sect's interpretation of the Lotus Sutra placed emphasis on the concept of "original enlightenment" (*hongaku* 本覚). Put simply, this concept states that the purpose of religious practice is not to attain enlightenment in the future, but to realize that one is already an enlightened being.

Saichō, the patriarch and founder of Tendai, established its spiritual home at Enryakuji temple in Mt Hiei in Kyoto in the late 8th century. In

805, he returned to Enryakuji with new Tiantai texts he had obtained from an extended stay in China sponsored by the Emperor. These texts along with esoteric scriptures, such as the Mahavairocana sutra, became the doctrinal source for Tendai Buddhism. However, Saichō's approach was pluralistic and he advocated the ideal of a Buddhist school based on the idea that all the teachings of the Buddha are without contradiction.

Saichō initially deepened his knowledge of Esoteric Buddhism with the cooperation and tutelage of Kūkai, but relations between the two later soured. Kūkai accused Saichō of carelessly promulgating esoteric Buddhist rites and teachings without fully understanding their deeper meanings. In turn, Saichō condemned Kūkai for denying the validity of transmitting the Dharma through writing, and insisting upon only the oral transmission of doctrines (see Abe, 1995).

ZEN (禅)

The meditative school of Zen Buddhism is traditionally recognized to have been first established in China in the sixth century by the enigmatic Buddhist monk known as Bodhidharma. Zen began to develop in Japan in the Kamakura period and split into two major sects: Rinzai and Sōtō. It is fair to say that Zen has produced some of the most brilliant and eccentric personalities in Japanese religious history. The major works and poetry of Zen masters such as Ikkyū, Hakuin and Dōgen have all been translated into English and they are essential reading for anyone with an interest in Zen philosophy.

Western conceptions of Zen have continued to be redefined since it first came to widespread public attention in the 1950s. The writings of D.T Suzuki (1870-1966) had a formative influence on the western interpretation of Zen Buddhist thought, but in the last few decades Suzuki's credentials as a "man of Zen" have been called into question by authors such as Robert Sharf, who asserted that Suzuki "remained a layman throughout his life" and most of his Zen training was "...squeezed into weekends and school vacations" (1993, p.12). Certainly, contradictory aspects within the popular conception of Zen Buddhism abound. It appears to be anti-traditionalist, yet with the transmission of the patriarchal robe, it emphasizes the importance of lineage and tradition. It is supposed to reject ritualism in favor of spontaneity yet, according to Sharf, "classical Zen ranks among the most ritualistic form of Buddhist monasticism" (1993, p.1).

In terms of its teaching and practices, Zen has developed its own particular doctrines and methods comparable to other Japanese Buddhist sects. The most well known of these include the practice of meditation (*zazen* 座禅), and the use of paradoxical questions (*kōan* 公案) to stimulate the disciple into experiencing awakening (*satori* 悟り). Unlike other Japanese Buddhist sects that developed in the Kamakura period, Zen maintained close links with its Chinese heritage so Zen temples also became centers for learning continental arts such as calligraphy, painting, poetry and the tea ceremony.

PURE LAND (*Jōdo shū* 浄土宗)

Pure Land Buddhism arrived in Japan in the 6th century. The essential practice in Pure Land Buddhism is to pay homage to Amithaba Buddha (Amida Nyorai) by piously chanting his name so that one will be reborn in the heavenly realm of the Pure Land. The chanting of a Buddha's name in this way is referred to as *nenbutsu* 念仏 (Buddha reflection). Elements of *nenbutsu* practice can also be found in other Buddhist sects but Pure Land insists that faith in Amida Nyorai is absolutely necessary and people cannot attain salvation on their own. This distinction classifies Pure Land as a *tariki* 他力(Other Power) sect, as opposed to a *jiriki* 自力 (Self-Power) sect such as Zen.

In the Heian period, the Pure Land vision was greatly promulgated by Genshin 源信 (942-1017), via his collection of essential teachings on Pure Land rebirth called *Ōjōyōshū*. This work, which describes the various forms of *nenbutsu* practice, became the initial authority for Pure Land followers. The next major figure in the Pure Land lineage was Hōnen (1133-1212). He further simplified Genshin's teachings and developed a concise and inclusive system that greatly appealed to the everyday Japanese folk. Compared with the arcane ritual complexities of Esoteric Buddhism, Hōnen's assertion that the simple practice of chanting Amida's name was worthy to attain salvation struck a chord with the masses and the Pure Land sect became a major movement.

Pure Land belief developed further under the influence of Shinran (1173-1263), a disciple of Hōnen. Shinran taught that *nenbutsu* practice should be carried out as a means of showing gratitude to Amida and not purely as a way to achieve rebirth in the Pure Land. In Shinran's view, traditional Buddhist practices were essentially egotistical, aimed at gaining merit and salvation. He sought to remove all the self-calculating aspects from religion and make the act of faith alone the true foundation for salvation. Shinran's teachings became the basis for the "True (Essence of the) Pure Land" sect" (Jōdo-shinshū 浄土真宗), which now has organizations all over the world.

NICHIREN BUDDHISM (Nichiren shū 日蓮宗)

Nichiren Buddhism refers to a wide range of Buddhist sects based on the teachings of the 13th century monk Nichiren (1222-1282). Like the charismatic founders of the Zen and Pure Land schools, Nichiren was originally trained in the aristocratic Mt Hiei Tendai tradition, but he left to bring his interpretation of the Buddhist teachings to the masses. Nichiren became convinced that the Buddha's supreme wisdom was to be found in the Lotus Sutra. He aimed to establish this Sutra as the sole source of ultimate authority and condemned other Buddhist teachings as false or inferior in an aggressive style of preaching known as *Shakubuku* 折伏, which means to "break and subdue". His vociferous and fiery rebukes to established sects and leaders (he called Kūkai "the prize liar of Japan") were not received well by the authorities and he was forced into exile several times.

Nichiren fervently believed that the Lotus Sutra was the only thing that could offer protection and salvation in a time of *mappō* 末法, the final age of the degeneration of the Buddha's law. The central practice for all forms of Nichiren Buddhism is the chanting of the *daimoku* mantra *"Namu-myōhō-renge-kyō"* (glory to the Lotus Sutra). Nichiren taught that chanting this mantra with requisite faith in the Lotus Sutra is the only way to assure true Buddhahood. In Nichiren Buddhism, Nichiren himself is deified as a reincarnation of the Buddha and the *daimoku* is viewed as the Dharma. Followers make pilgrimages to the head temple of the Nichiren **Shōshu** school of Buddhism at Taisekiji, near Fujinomiya City in Shizuoka Prefecture, where the ashes of Nichiren are kept.

Several years after Nichiren's death, various schools and temples were established in his name with different adaptations of his teachings. These days, there are over thirty branches in the Nichiren lineage and, unlike other Buddhist sects, their members actively proselytize. It is worth mentioning that Nichiren Buddhism gave rise to the Soka Gakkai organisation which exerts considerable influence on the political establishment in Japan through its political wing the *Kōmeitō* 公明党.

はじめに
INTRODUCTION

The Thirteen Buddha Rites (*jūsan butsuji* 十三仏事) are a series of funeral rites and premortem offerings made to thirteen Buddhist deities on specific dates that have become strongly affiliated with the Shingon sect of Esoteric Buddhism in Japan. The exact origin of these rites and their historical development has yet to be seriously addressed in western scholarship, and although Japanese studies on the subject are more numerous, it still remains an emerging field in the study of Japanese religious practice.

The term "Thirteen Buddhas" is somewhat deceptive as the group is made up of five Buddhas (*nyorai* 如来), seven Bodhisattvas (*bosatsu* 菩薩) and one Wisdom King (*Myō-ō* 明王). Only the historical Buddha Shaka Nyorai (Sakyamuni) is accepted as a person; the others are essentially metaphysical concepts, similar to the archetypes or forms of Platonism. In terms of hierarchal status, the Buddhas are the most exalted deities and they are the main figures paid worship to by the various Buddhist sects in Japan. For example, the cosmological Buddha Dainichi Nyorai (Mahavairocana) is the main deity of the Shingon sect, the Pure Land sects venerate Amida Nyorai and generally the Zen sects pay homage to Shaka Nyorai. Bodhisattvas are associated with the Mahayana Buddhist teachings and they are best described as enlightened beings who, seeing the profound contradiction in attaining Nirvana only for themselves, consent to be reborn again until all suffering beings attain Buddhahood. The Wisdom Kings (also translated as "Kings of Light", "Mantra Kings" etc.) were originally Hindu deities who were later adopted into the Japanese esoteric sects. From the thirteenth century, they were transformed from esoteric deities to popular protector gods, guarding against evil forces. Fudō Myō-ō is by far the most prevalent Wisdom King in Japan followed by his counterpart the "Wisdom King of Lust" Aizen Myō-ō 愛染明王.

Rituals centred around thirteen Buddhist deities are unique to Japan and are closely connected with memorial services for the deceased. Bishop Taisen Miyata of the Shingon sect describes a typical memorial service as follows:

> "…[T]he thirteen deities are regarded as the guardians of specific days after the death of a loved one. On certain days after the death, the family and friends of the deceased gather in front of a scroll depicting the thirteen deities, and there a memorial service is held. […] On the memorial day, the family and friends of the deceased gather around a scroll or pictorial representation of all of the above thirteen deities, and there each mantra is recited. This pious custom is even today still practiced in many parts of Japan."

In the Shingon sect, each of the thirteen deities has their own individual mantra made up of three parts: an introductory syllable such as *om* (Jp on); a short description of the deity; and a closing syllable which is usually the Sanskrit seed syllable (*shuji* 種子) unique to each deity. The recital of this seed syllable is believed to call forth the Buddhist deity to arise in either the practitioner's mental or physical vision. In this sense, the mantras are recited with the belief in the mystical power of sound to unite the practitioner with the invoked deity. Although the use of these specific mantras is mostly restricted to the esoteric Buddhist sects, the Thirteen Buddha series of mortuary rites became standard at most Buddhist temples by the middle of the Edo period. At the heart of these rites lies the belief that the Buddhas can be petitioned to provide help and assistance to the deceased's spirit as it journeys into the afterlife.

In Buddhism, each sentient being has a number of lives and deaths that follow on from each other in an almost unending cycle (the attainment of nirvana being considered a rare event). As one life leads to another, the gap between death and rebirth became an issue of considerable concern. By holding feasts or making various offerings to the Buddhist deities according to specific memorial days, it is believed that one can gain merit that will be transferred to aid the departed before reincarnation (a concept known in Japan as *tsuizen kuyō* 追善供養). The Thirteen Buddha Rites, however, from their inception, extended beyond Buddhist funerary memorial services to include premortem offerings known as *gyakushu* 逆修. These are actions carried out to increase one's own store of merit in preparation for one's own death. For modern Japanese, the practice of undertaking premortem rituals at temples and sites related to the Thirteen Buddhas has largely become a popular form of pilgrimage or sightseeing known as *jūsanbutsu reijō* 十三仏霊場. There are currently at least twenty designated Thirteen Buddha pilgrimage sites operating across Japan. At some locations, Japanese bus companies even run special routes, usually on the thirteenth day of the month, stopping at thirteen different temples—one for each of the deities.

To understand how the Thirteen Buddha Rites came to be, it is important to try to locate their place within the larger historical development of Japanese premortem and postmortem rituals. Surviving written documents from the early Heian period record postmortem rituals conducted by the elite members of Japanese society as far back as the eighth century. It was believed that these rituals, if done properly, enabled the living to transfer merit to restore the karmic balance of the soul as it passed through the crucial forty-nine day period after death. I begin by drawing from some of the earliest written records of these rituals found in courtiers diaries commonly referred to as *kanbun nikki* 漢文日記. Here we find written evidence that these forty-nine days— divided into seven periods of seven days— were associated with various Buddhist deities for both postmortem and premortem rituals known as the "seven seventh-day rites". Despite the existence of such practices in medieval Japan, most scholarship on the Thirteen Buddha Rites attributes their origin to the Chinese belief in the Ten Kings of Hell that was brought to Japan around the twelfth century. I investigate this belief in chapter two and discuss how *The Scripture on the Ten Kings of*

Hell redefined the afterlife as a kind of bureaucratic purgatory. In chapter 3, we shall see how the Bodhisattva Jizō's identification as the alter ego of Enma ō (the judge of the dead) made him an essential element in the interpretation of the Ten Kings as manifestations of Buddhist deities, made explicit in *The Scripture on Jizō and the Ten Kings*. I then conclude the analysis of written documents in chapter 4 with a discussion on an important apocryphal scripture known as the *Kōbō Daishi Gyakushu nikkinokoto* 弘法大師逆修日記事. This provided the template for the Thirteen Buddha Rites by extending the period for postmortem rites to thirty-three years after death, and standardizing the selection, order and number of Buddhist deities, which had hitherto been quite varied. It was also one of the earliest written records to include dates for premortem worship, and I shall reveal how the selection of these dates were influenced by some obscure beliefs and traditions known as the *sanjūnichi hibutsu* 三十日密仏 and the *jūsainichi shinkō* 十斎日信仰.

Due to the lack of written sources available, researchers have only been able to speculate theories about the reasons why three more deities were added to the Ten Kings and the period of worship extended from three to thirty-three years after death. This has led to a number of interesting theories on the importance of some of the numerological correspondences of the Thirteen Buddha Rites, and some intriguing ideas concerning the esoteric meaning of the rites which I discuss in detail in chapter 5. Part two focuses on the archaeological evidence of stone memorials and sites related to Thirteen Buddha rituals and worship. I have chosen a selection of monuments and steles that illustrate a transitional period between the worship of the Ten Kings and the Thirteen Buddhas. I shall demonstrate how some of these monuments predate the earliest written documents on the Thirteen Buddha Rites, and seek to explain what this tells us about their historical development. In sum, the main objective of this investigation is to provide a chronology of the historical development of the rites, draw attention to their influences and origins, and point to some areas for future study.

十三仏の紹介
INTRODUCING THE THIRTEEN BUDDHAS

I refer to the Thirteen Buddhas throughout using their romanicized Japanese titles, but I have included their Sanskrit names in brackets in the following descriptions as a reference for those readers more familiar with those denominations. The individual mantras for each deity have been adapted from the studies of Arai (2003, p.77-84) and Miyata (2006, p.9-22). They are given in the following order (top to bottom): Sanskrit, Japanese, English.

It can be difficult to tell many of the deities apart from each other in their various representations in paintings and sculptures, but most have certain unique iconographical characteristics that help to identify them. As a general rule, Buddhas are usually dressed in simple garments and they do not wear crowns (Dainichi aside) or carry weapons. All of the deities have certain symbolic hand gestures (mudras), which they are associated with, and I include a brief description of the key ones to look out for where applicable. However, as multiple deities sometimes use the same or similar mudras, it is not always possible to accurately identify them using these alone.

Fudō-Myō-ō 不動明王 (Acala)

Premortem date of worship: sixteenth day of the first month.
Postmortem date of worship: seven days after death.

"*Namah samanta-vajranām hām*"
"*Naumaku sanmanda bazara dan senda makaroshada sowataya untarata kanman*"
"*Homage to all the deities of vajra rank, especially those whose seed syllable is hām*"

Fudō Myō-ō, "The Immovable King of Light", was first introduced to Japan by Kūkai (779-835), the founder of Shingon Buddhism. Fudō is a translation of the Sanskrit Acala, which means "not moving". Although his immovability is often interpreted to represent fortitude and obstinacy (compounded by the rock by which he stands), the Zen scholar D.T. Suzuki suggested that it refers to the immovable intelligence of the mind remaining forever tranquil and yet mobile all the time.

His fearsome appearance belies his compassion for sentient beings: he uses the sword in his right hand to destroy evil desires, ignorance, pride; in his left hand he carries a binding rope to discipline the mind and draw beings in towards liberation. Surrounded by flames symbolizing the metaphysical knowledge which burns ignorance, he remains the deity most commonly invoked in the goma fire purification rituals performed in the esoteric sects. However, perhaps because of his lightning-like sword, he has also been the focal point of many mystical rain-making rituals.

Fudō is viewed to be an alter ego of Dainichi Nyorai so consequently he can often be seen standing in the vicinity of Dainichi in paintings and sculptures. Offerings are made to him on the seventh day after death in order that he will come to pacify the minds of the recently deceased.

Shaka Nyorai 釈迦如来   (Sakyamuni)

Premortem date: twenty-ninth day of the second month.

Postmortem date: fourteen days after death.

"Namah samanta-buddhanām bhah"

"Naumaku sanmanda bodanan baku"

"Homage to the Buddhas, especially those whose seed syllable is bhah"

Shaka is the Japanese name for Sakyamuni (Sage of the Shaka Clan), the historical Buddha on whose teachings Buddhism was founded. Born in present day Nepal in either the mid-6th or mid-5th century B.C., he left behind a life of privilege to become a mendicant ascetic at 29 years old, and 6 years later attained enlightenment, thereby becoming a Buddha or 'enlightened one'.

It was originally deemed inappropriate to depict the actual form of the Buddha in human form, so instead he was represented by symbols such as the Wheel of the Law (Dharmacakra), the lotus flower, the conch shell and the Bodhi tree. The first anthropomorphic images started to appear in the Christian era, and it was said that the form of his body was borrowed from the wide breast and narrow waist of the lion and the head from the bull, while the eyes recall the lotus bud, the eyebrows the Indian bow, and the three folds of the neck the undulations of the conch shell.

Two of the most common hand gestures associated with Shaka are the "Fear not Mudra" (right hand held up), a gesture that symbolizes the granting of protection to Buddhist followers, and the "Exposition of the Dharma Mudra" (featured in the illustration) which is the mudra he used when preaching his first sermon after reaching enlightenment. Significantly, the hands are held in front of the heart in this mudra, symbolizing that the Buddha's teachings come straight from the heart.

Monju-bosatsu 文殊菩薩 (Manjusri)

Premortem date: twenty-fifth day of the third month.

Postmortem date: twenty-one days after death.

mam

"Om a ra pa ca na"

"On arahashanō"

"Homage to arahashano"

Monju is a Bodhisattva of wisdom. Wisdom is a concept derived from *prajnā,* and can be broadly defined within Buddhism to refer to right cognition: the understanding of the absence of a permanent, abiding self in all things. He often carries a sword in his right hand to sever the roots of ignorance and aid all beings to awakening; in his left hand he either holds a scroll which represents the Perfection of Wisdom Sutra (*hannya kyō* 般若経), or a lotus flower which symbolizes the pure, undefiled Buddha mind.

Monju is often depicted with five curls in his hair and there are also five syllables in his mantra if the honorific "On" is omitted. In specific relation to Monju, five represents the five wisdom peaks of *Godaisan* 五台山, his holy mountain in China, which to this day remains a popular place for Buddhist pilgrimages.

Monju and Fugen are often portrayed either side of Shaka in a grouping known as the Shaka trinity or triad (*Shaka sanzon* 釈迦三尊). Monju is usually positioned on the left side on top of a lion holding a sword—a style of Monju first introduced to Japan in the Heian era by the Tendai Buddhist monk Ennin. The word "arahashano" in Monju's mantra "homage to arahashano" is the name of an Indian alphabet. Since Monju symbolizes both learning and transcendental wisdom, it is appropriate to his mantra.

Fugen-bosatsu 普賢菩薩 (Samanthabhadra)

Premortem date: fourteenth day of the fourth month.

Postmortem date: twenty-eight days after death.

am

"Om samayas tvam"

"On sanmaya satoban"

"You are one (with the Buddhas)"

Fugen represents the virtues of meditation and diligent practice. He is venerated for the ten vows or resolutions he took to obtain enlightenment which have become common practice in East Asian Buddhism. He is ordinarily portrayed sitting on top of a white elephant with six tusks. The elephant symbolises the strength of Buddhism to overcome all obstacles and the six tusks represent the six fields: sight, sound, scent, taste, touch and concepts (of the mind).

Though originally male, and often featuring a moustache, Fugen came to have a feminine appearance and represent the ideal of feminine beauty. He is often depicted alongside Monju, but whereas Monju is the patron of the transcendental wisdom gained at the end of one's religious quest, Fugen is the patron of the religious quest itself.

He is portrayed in the Womb World Mandala holding a three-pronged vajra in his left hand which rests upon a lotus flower. Within esoteric and other forms of tantric-based Buddhism, the vajra is often paired with the lotus as representing two aspects of a single (non-dual) reality. In other representations, Fugen is sometimes seen with both hands pressed together in prayer or with his right hand palm facing up with three fingers outstretched (see picture). The three fingers represent the three forms of conduct: thoughts, words and actions, each of which respectively form the "three mysteries" of esoteric Buddhism: Meditation, Mantra and Mudra.[1]

Jizō-bosatsu 地蔵菩薩　(Ksitigarbha)

Premortem date: twenty-fourth day of the fifth month.

Postmortem date: thirty five days after death.

"Om ha-ha-ha vismaye svāhā"

"On ka ka ka bisanmaei sowaka"

"Ha ha ha! Hail to him in his majesty"

The much-loved Jizō rose to prominence in Japan at the end of the Heian period and he is widely regarded as a Bodhisattva of compassion. However, his role has changed considerably through the ages: from saviour and guide, to protector of travellers and women in childbirth. These days, he is most widely seen as the protector of children and it is common to see statues of Jizō at temples adorned with red bibs and caps which were said to have been worn by children in earlier times. Women who have had a miscarriage, stillbirth or abortion, will often visit temples and pay their respects to Jizō in a kind of fetus memorial service known as *mizuko kuyō* 水子供養.

Jizō has a number of feminine traits, and in a previous existence he was said to have been a woman. He holds a wish giving pearl in his left hand that represents the effulgence of Buddhist doctrine, and carries a staff with six rings that symbolize the six realms of reincarnation. Groups of six Jizō statues (see below) are commonly found outside Buddhist temples or placed at busy intersections for the protection of travelers.

Miroku-bosatsu 弥勒菩薩　(Maitreya)

Premortem date: fifteenth day of the sixth month.

Postmortem date: forty-two days after death.

"Om Maitreya svāhā"

"On maitareiya sowaka"

"Hail to thee, compassionate one"

The Thirteen Buddhas

The cult of Miroku entered Japan in the early sixth century and developed into two basic motifs: a motif of ascent (*jōsho* 上生) and a motif of descent (*geshō* 下生). In the former, Miroku is believed to be residing in Tusita heaven (*tosotsuten* 兜率天) a place of rebirth for devotees who have acquired enough merit. In the descent motif, Miroku is the messianic Buddha of the future, who will one day come to earth to put an end to the sufferings of the virtuous and restore true religion. It is a commonly held belief by the followers of Shingon Buddhism that their leader Kūkai did not die and merely entered a state of suspended life at Mt Kōya where he awaits Miroku's descent.

The earliest depictions of Miroku such as the wood carving displayed at Chūgūji (see p.106), show a relaxed, contemplative posture implying both the ease and elegance of Miroku's paradise and his pondering how to save all the beings in the world. In other representations, Miroku is shown seated cross-legged holding a lotus flower in his right hand with a small vase of water resting upon it containing an elixir of wisdom.

Some scholars have suggested that Miroku's messianic qualities contradict the need for self-effort to attain enlightenment, stressed by the Buddha himself. However, if we view Miroku's paradise as the emanation of a world after all human beings have fully integrated the teachings of the Buddha into their lives, there is no discernible contradiction.

Yakushi Nyorai 薬師如来　(Bhaisajya-guru)

Premortem date: eighth day of the seventh month.

Postmortem date: forty-nine days after death.

bhai

"Om huru huru candali matangi svāhā"

"On koro koro sendari matōgi sowaka"

"Hail to thee, Candāli and Mātangi"

Yakushi is the medicine Buddha, the doctor of souls and bodies. He holds a pot of medicine in one hand, to heal the sicknesses of body and mind, and he is sometimes flanked either side by the Bodhisattvas of the sun and moon (Nikkō and Gakkō), perhaps because the early practice of medicine was associated with solar and lunar principles. He is typically shown seated with the palm of his right hand raised in the "Fear not Mudra" but on rare occasions he may be observed with both hands lying in his lap, thumbs together, palms up supporting the pot of medicine. The pot contains a balm to cure the blindness of ignorance and awaken the True Eye of Dharma.

Yakushi assumes the seventh position in the Thirteen Buddha Rites; a number which has been associated with him since the medieval period as he was believed to manifest in seven forms (*shichibutsu yakushi* 七仏薬師). He is also affiliated with the number twelve for the twelve vows he made as a Bodhisattva, **and** upon the fulfillment of these vows he became the Lord of the Eastern Paradise of Pure Lapis Lazuli (*jōruri* 浄瑠璃). Yakushi and his scriptures are protected by **Twelve Heavenly Generals (*jūnishinshō* 十二神将).** These twelve protective deities became associated with the twelve animals of the Chinese Zodiac and I discuss their relationship with Yakushi in more detail in chapter 5.

Kannon-bosatsu 観音菩薩　(Avalokitesvara)

Premortem date: eighteenth day of the eighth month

Postmortem date: one hundred days after death.

sa

"*Om! Alolik svāhā*"

"*On arorikya sowaka*"

"*Hail to the lord of the lotus rank deities*"

Kannon (the one who sees/hears all), also referred to as Kanzeon 観世音, is best conceptualized as the Bodhisattva of mercy. Understood to protect living beings with loving compassion, Kannon remains one of the most popular Buddhist deities in Japan. The faithful are promised that Kannon will shatter the sword of the executioner, grant the birth of sons and enable someone who has fallen from a high cliff to hang suspended in midair.

Kannon presides over an island mountain paradise called Fudaraku (補陀落) considered to be a Pure Land accessible from the Earthly Realm (the location is most commonly placed near the southern tip of India which suggests a south Indian origin for this deity). Vowing to continually work for the salvation of sentient beings, Kannon is said to appear in thirty-three different forms. The deity also has a further six esoteric or tantric forms, one being the six-armed Nyoirin Kannon whose duty is to save all sentient beings trapped in the Six Realms of Reincarnation.

Originally male in appearance, Kannon is now often portrayed as a female in Japan assuming the archetypal attributes of the divine mother goddess. Most commonly, Kannon is represented wearing a crown and holding a lotus or a water vase. The eighteenth day of each month is considered Kannon's holy day (*ennichi* 縁日), so fittingly the premortem rite date for Kannon is the eighteenth of August.

Seishi-bosatsu 勢至菩薩 (Mahasthamaprapta)

Premortem date: twenty-third day of the ninth month.

Postmortem date: one year after death.

sah

"*Om sam jam jam sah svāhā*"

"*On sanzansaku sowaka*"

(This mantra is made up of symbolic syllables only and eludes English translation)

Seishi bosatsu, also known as Dai (Great) Seishi meaning "he who has attained great strength", is one of the lesser well-known and worshipped deities of the Thirteen Buddhas. It is very rare to find him depicted alone in Buddhist art and he is mostly only recognized as part of the Amida triad where he is often positioned on the right side of Amida with his hands pressed together in front of his chest in the "praying hands" pose.

The late esoteric philosopher Manly.P.Hall explained the Amida trinity as an allegory of the spiritual, mental and generative powers of the Sun; represented anatomically in the heart, mind and reproductive system. According to his interpretation, Seishi (the physical aspect) and Kannon (the mental aspect) become reflexes or expressions of Amida, the spiritual solar logos. A more traditional interpretation suggests Seishi represents the masculine attribute of knowledge or wisdom working in contradistinction to the feminine grace of Kannon while Amida stands for the Buddha nature in sentient beings.

In memorial services, offerings are made to Seishi one year after death. As this may be a time when the bereaved families diligence to perform the rites has subsided, the light and wisdom of Seishi (symbolized by his crown ornamented with a small vase of water) is believed to rejuvenate their compassion.

Amida Nyorai 阿弥陀如来 (Amithaba)

Premortem date: fifteenth day of the tenth month.

Postmortem date: three years after death.

hrih

"Om! Amrta-teje hara hūm"

"On Amirita teisei kara un"

"Save us in the glory of the Deathless One"

Amida, the Buddha of "Immeasurable Light", is the central deity of the Pure Land sects which came to prominence in Japan in the Kamakura era and remain some of the nation's largest and most popular. Amida faith is predominantly concerned with the after-life, and those who call his name and meditate on his characteristics are said to be reborn in the Western Paradise of Ultimate Bliss (*gokuraku jyōdo* 極楽浄土) where Amida resides. This doctrine was denounced vociferously by influential Buddhist figures such as Nichiren (1222-1282) and Hakuin (1686-1768), who stressed that the Pure Land existed within one's own mind and could only be discovered through diligent practice and meditation.

Welcoming approach (*Raigō* 来迎) paintings of Amida descending from paradise on a purple cloud to receive a believer at the time of death are renowned in Buddhist art. In other representations, Amida may be displayed seated or standing, paired with another Buddha or as the central part of a triad. He holds no defining attributes but is usually portrayed performing one of three main mudras. The Meditation Mudra (*zenjōin* 禅定印),where his hands rest on his lap, is most famously displayed in the large statue of Amida in Kamakura. The Mudra of the Exposition of the Dharma (*Seppōin* 説法印) shows both hands pointing upwards, thumb and forefingers pressed together. Finally, as shown in the picture opposite, the Welcoming Mudra (*Raigōin* 来迎印), has the right hand raised, left hand lowered with the thumb touching one of three fingers.

Ashuku Nyorai 阿閦如来 (Aksobhya)

Premortem date: fifteenth day of the eleventh month.

Postmortem date: seven years after death.

hūm

"Om! Aksobhya hūm"

"On Akishubiya un"

"Oh Immovable One, Hūm"

Ashuku is the Buddha of the Pure Land in the East: *Zenke* 善快— the Land of Great Pleasure. His Japanese name is a translation of the Sanskrit *Aksobhya* (the immovable or unshakeable one) and refers to his even temperament. According to Buddhist scripture, Ashuku made a vow to generate no thoughts of anger or malice until he attained enlightenment. He has a high status within esoteric sects as one of the four Buddhas that guard Dainichi Nyorai in the perfected body assembly (*jōjine* 成身会) of the Diamond World Mandala. This mandala is a central component of the esoteric Buddhist teachings, and it is perhaps best explained as a kind of encoded map used in conjunction with the Womb World Mandala to navigate the practitioner towards union with cosmological reality.

Ashuku's iconographical characteristic is the Earth-Touching Mudra (*shokuchi-in* 触地印) which symbolizes his spiritual immovability. His left hand either lies in his lap clenched to form the "adamantine fist" (*kongōken* 金剛拳), or it may hold a corner of his robe. The latter gesture signifies his determination to support and encourage others to attain enlightenment.

Dainichi Nyorai 大日如来 (Mahavairocana)

Premortem date: twenty-eighth day of the eleventh month.

Postmortem date: thirteen years after death.

vam

"Om Vajra-dhātu Vam"

"On abiraunken bazara dadoban"

"Hail to the Diamond realm"

Dainichi Nyorai, the primordial cosmic Buddha of the Shingon sect, represents the life energy of the universe: the source from which all the other Buddhas and Bodhisattvas are brought into being. The Shingon scholar Taiko Yamazaki stated that he might have originated from the deity known in the Vedas as Asura, which in turn seems to be related to the Zoroastrian Ahura Mazda, god of light. However, it is important to point out that unlike other solar deities, Dainichi represents the inborn life-energy of the universe, and is therefore the Sun that never sets.

He is often portrayed clasping the forefinger of his left hand with his right, in a mudra known as the Wisdom Fist (*chiken-in* 智拳印). The five fingers of the right hand represent the five material elements (earth, water, fire, wind, space) and the index finger of the left hand represents the sixth element: mind or consciousness. According to Shingon cosmology, just as human beings consist of five material elements and a spiritual element (mind), so too does Dainichi consist of an enlightened mind and body. The interlinked hands demonstrate the interpenetrability of the Diamond and Womb World Mandalas and their unification signifies the inseparability of the microcosm and the macrocosm.

虚空蔵菩薩 Kokūzō-bosatsu (Akasagarbha)

Premortem date: thirteenth day of the twelfth month.

Postmortem date: thirty-three years after death.

trāh

"Namo ākasa gharbaya om mali kamali mauli svāhā"

"Naubō akyasyakyarabaya onarikya maribori sowaka"

"All hail the august womb of emptiness who holds flower, lotus and jewel crown"

The thirteenth and final deity is the Bodhisattva Kokūzō, the "Womb of Emptiness" or "Storehouse of Wisdom", who symbolises unlimited wisdom and compassion and is believed to be able to grant all wishes. More esoterically, he represents the fifth element: ether or space—the highest of the first five elements (See DeVisser, p.10). He also represents the planet Venus in the Shingon ritual the *gumonjihō* 求聞持法, a prolonged mantra recital and meditation practice believed to bestow the devoted practitioner with the boon of supernatural memory.

Kokūzō is typically shown holding a sword in his right hand, and a lotus flower in his left on which is placed a precious jewel. As the thirteenth deity, Kokūzō is intimately connected with the number thirteen. His premortem date is the thirteenth of the twelfth month and on the Japanese island of Honshu, children who are thirteen years of age pay homage to Kokūzō in the hopes of becoming more intelligent. In postmortem rituals, Kokūzō marks the thirty-third year of death. The number thirty-three signifies a stage of ascension or transformation and in the context of the Thirteen Buddha rites it marks the point in time when the deceased attains Nirvanic salvation or reincarnation. Formal offerings and services from surviving family members are no longer required after the thirty-third year and the Thirteen Buddha Rites come to their completion.

PART ONE

十三仏の文献

THE THIRTEEN BUDDHA RITES IN SCRIPTURE

… The Thirteen Buddhas

Chapter One

七七斎

SEVEN SEVENTH-DAY RITES

One of the earliest written records of memorial offerings made in Japan comes from a passage in the *Shoku Nihongi* 続日本紀, an imperially commissioned historical record completed in 797 AD, covering the 95 year period from the beginning of Emperor Mommu's reign in 697. In a diary entry dated 735, Emperor Shōmu makes reference to the seven seventh-days after death (*shichi shichisai* 七七斎) — forty nine days of mourning that included offerings to facilitate the transfer of merit to the deceased. In order to give the Thirteen Buddha Rites a sense of historical perspective, it is necessary to explain in more detail the significance of these seven seventh-day rites. Students of comparative religion will be aware of the recurrence of the number seven across numerous religious texts and ancient myths.[2] However, the explicit connection of seven seventh-day rites with an intermediate state of existence (*chū'u* 中有) derives from Buddhism. Stephen Teiser notes that even before the development of the Mahāyāna schools, several sects of Indian Buddhism espoused the idea of an intermediate existence between death and rebirth. The opportunity for beings to escape this liminal stage was believed to occur only once every seven days and then only under favorable karmic circumstances (Teiser, 1994, p.23).

We find reference to the crucial period of forty-nine days in *The Tibetan Book of the Dead*. The Tibetan text describes and guides the deceased through the journey of consciousness during the interval between death and the next rebirth known as the bardo. From Evans-Wentz's translation:

> "There will be a grey twilight-like light, both by night and by day, and at all times. In that kind of Intermediate State thou wilt be either for one, two, three, four, five, six, or seven weeks, until the forty-ninth day."

In the Heian era (794-1185 A.D), we start to see evidence of memorial services connecting these forty-nine days with specific Buddhist deities in records such as the diary of Taira no Nobunori (*Hyōhanki* 兵範記), which covers the period from 1132 to 1171. The following memorial service for Emperor Toba is recorded in table 1 as follows:

22nd day of the 12th month	Yakushi	7 days
29th day of the 12th month	Kokūzō	14 days
7th day of the 1st month	Monju	21 days
14th day of the 1st month	Jizō	28 days
21st day of the 1st month	Shaka triad	35 days
28th day of the 1st month	No Buddha listed	42 days
5th day of the 2nd month	Amida	49 days

Table 1: Extract from the *Hyōhanki* 兵範記

Although all of the deities listed here are also members of the Thirteen Buddhas, there appears to be no correlation between their order and dates. The only conclusion we can infer from it is that the presence of Amida as the seventh Buddha most likely resulted from the strong influence of the Pure Land sect during this period. Followers of the Pure Land school, particularly before the rise of Hōnen (1133-1212) and Shinran (1173-1262), believed that those who could focus their thoughts on the Buddha at the time of death would be welcomed by Amida himself and escorted to the Western Paradise of Ultimate Bliss. Seen in this context, the placement of Amida as the final Buddha was likely instigated as a means to propagate Pure Land belief and doctrine.

The first written records documenting the worship of Buddhist deities for premortem services also seem to appear around the late Heian era. Watanabe compares accounts of premortem seven seventh-day rites found in courtiers recorded diaries, revealing that the practice of using

Buddhist deities for these rites was well established in the elite and aristocratic circles as far back as the twelfth century. I reproduce Watanabe's summary of the following premortem rites recorded in the *Hyōhanki* 兵範記 and the *Chūyūki* 中有記[3] in table 2 below to illustrate the variations in the types of *honzon* worshipped.

Period of time	List of deities as recorded in a diary entry dated 1134.	List of deities as recorded in a diary entry dated 1252.	List of deities as recorded in a diary entry dated 1269.
7 days	Amida	Amida	Yakushi
14 days	Injō Mandala (迎接曼荼羅)	Kannon	Miroku
21 days	Miroku	Yakushi	Thousand-armed Kannon
28 days	Nyoirin Kannon	Kokūzō	Jizō
35 days	Jizō	Shaka	Shaka
42 days	Kokūzō	Fugen	Fudō
49 days	Shaka	Jizō	Fugen

Table 2: Extracts from the *Hyōhanki* 兵範記 and *Chūyūki* 中有記 referenced in Watanabe, 1989, p.172-173.

It is important to note that although these seven seventh-day rites list the period of time from seven to forty-nine days, in reality they were conducted over a much shorter time span—anything from seven days to within half a month. This kind of flexibility in the ritual practice is also noticeable in the diverse choice of the main deities (*honzon* 本尊) which do not seem to follow any prescribed pattern. Shaka, Jizō and Kannon are the only deities to appear in all three services so one can only surmise that certain *honzon* were selected in accord with sectarian beliefs. The order of the Buddhist deities would start to become more standardized after *The Scripture of Jizō and the Ten Kings* became widespread, which I discuss in chapter three.

The Thirteen Buddhas

Chapter Two

預修十王生七経
THE SCRIPTURE ON THE TEN KINGS

The Scripture on the Ten Kings (Yoshu jūō shō shichi kyō 預修十王生七経) is attributed to an obscure Chinese figure known only as Tsang-ch'uan (藏川) and is believed to have been compiled sometime between 756 and the early tenth century. The scripture portrays the deceased as a prisoner having their soul examined in a trial administered by ten kings (or judges), each in turn. The first seven kings cover the period of seven weeks, and the final three extend the memorial dates to the hundredth day, the first month after the full year, and the third year after death. The English names for each king and the judgment dates are listed in the following order, shown in Table 3 opposite (romanized versions of the Japanese names are shown in brackets).

The Thirteen Buddhas

Order of Service	King of Hell	Time after death
1	King Kuang of Ch'in (*Shinkō ō*)	7 days
2	King of the First River (*Shokō ō*)	14 days
3	King Ti if Sung (*Sōtei ō*)	21 days
4	King of the Five Offices (*Gokan ō*)	28 days
5	King Yama rāja (*Enma ō*)	35 days
6	King of Transformations (*Hensei ō*)	42 days
7	King of Mount T'ai (*Taizan ō*)	49 days
8	Impartial King (*Byōdō ō*)	100 days
9	King of the Capital (*Toshi ō*)	1 year
10	King Who Turns the Wheel of Rebirth in the Five Paths (*Godō Tenrin ō*)	3 years

Table 3: Ten Kings of Hell

After hearing the judgment of the previous four Kings, King Yama, known in Japan as Enma ō 閻魔王, sentences the defendant on the thirty-fifth day to be reborn in one of Six Realms of Reincarnation (*rokudō* 六道). Those whose actions were deemed to be good are reborn in one of the three higher paths as a god, a human or a titanlike being (*ashura* 阿修羅). Others are condemned to hell or forced to relive life as an animal or hungry ghost. *The Scripture on the Ten Kings* maintains that release can be obtained if the grieving family sends offerings to each of the Ten Kings at the appropriate time. Further, it was thought to be even more beneficial to send offerings to the Ten Kings on one's own behalf while still living. In China, such offerings were made as far back as the ninth century in the form of ten feast days in accordance with the schedule outlined in *The Scripture on the Ten Kings*.[4] In later days, priests were paid a sum of money to make a copy of the scripture for the benefit of the commissioner. Thus, *The Scripture on the Ten Kings*, promoted both postmortem offerings made by relatives of the deceased as well as premortem rituals dedicated to the Ten Kings to ensure a propitious rebirth.

Photo of the Ten Kings of Hell taken from the Jūōdo in Nozawa Onsen (note Jizō's position on the left side of Enma Ō).

The Thirteen Buddhas

Chapter Three

地蔵十王経

THE SCRIPTURE ON JIZŌ AND THE TEN KINGS

The eastward transmission of the rituals, art and literature of the Ten Kings to Japan is believed to have first taken place sometime between the 12th and 13th centuries. It is then thought that the belief began to spread through Japan via the funerary rites and practices of Buddhist priests affiliated with the Pure Land sect. They would later become a customary part of the funerary practice of the Shingon, Tendai, Zen and Nichiren traditions.

Although the Ten Kings were not originally conceived as Buddhist deities, Jizō was often a central figure in many of the pictures and artworks of the Ten Kings imported to Japan in the early Heian period. To be able to understand this, we need to take into consideration Jizō's interpretation as an alter ego of King Yama. In many of the paintings of the courts of the Ten Kings produced in medieval Japan, Jizō is often superimposed above the fifth court of hell to demonstrate his role as the twin of King Yama. Such an association suggested that other kings could also potentially be seen as manifestations of Buddhist deities, and this view was made explicit in *The Scripture on Jizō and the Ten Kings* (地蔵十王経)[5]. Like *The Scripture on the Ten Kings*, it outlines the journey of the deceased's spirit through ten courts of purgatory. The real importance of this text for our study is that it appears to be the earliest written record that pairs the Ten Kings with Buddhist deities. This is commonly referred to as an example of *honji suijaku* 本地垂迹— a kind of assimilation process where the Ten Kings are seen as traces (*suijaku*), or alternative incarnations of the original Buddhas. To date, no existing record in Chinese literature has been found that similarly links the Ten Kings to Buddhist deities, making this a distinctly Japanese phenomenon[6]. Watanabe cross references it with Japanese records such as the *Jijūhyakuinenshū* 私聚百因縁集[7] compiled in 1257, and the *Hōbutsushū* 宝物集[8] dated 1179, and deducts that it was composed sometime between the later half of the twelfth and the early half of the thirteenth century. The Buddhas and kings are listed in the following order with a memorial schedule of seven seven-day periods plus the one-hundredth day, one year, and three-year observances (see table 4).

Buddhist Deity	King of Hell	Time after death
1. Fudō	Shinkō ō	7 days
2. Shaka	Shokō ō	14 days
3. Monju	Sōtei ō	21 days
4. Fugen	Gokan ō	28 days
5. Jizō	Enma ō	35 days
6. Miroku	Hensei ō	42 days
7. Yakushi	Taizan ō	49 days
8. Kannon	Byōdō ō	100 days
9. Ashuku	Toshi ō	1 year
10. Amida	Godō Tenrin ō	3 years

Table 4: List of deities recorded in *The Scripture on Jizō and the Ten Kings*

Despite being the earliest text linking the Ten Kings with equivalent Buddhist deities (and therefore logically the source reference for later texts), researchers have not found any other reproduction of this exact allocation in Japanese medieval records. To demonstrate the extent of the disparities, Shimizu cites an example from the *Futsūshōdōshū* 普通唱導集 compiled in 1297, where half of the Buddhist deities are listed in a different order from those in *The Scripture on the Ten Kings*. There are also more systematic variations in the selection of the ten Buddhist deities in the earliest records of the Pure Land and Shingon schools that clearly show how certain Buddhas important to each sect were prioritized. For example, Pure Land scriptures such as the *Hyakuinenshū* 百因縁集 feature the Amida triad (Kannon, Seishi, Amida) as the final three deities, and Shingon records often allocate Dainichi to the tenth position. The only real consistency throughout the medieval records appears to be the placement of Jizō as the *honjibutsu* for Enma ō who is regularly located in fifth place.

Chapter Four

弘法大師逆修日記事
KŌBŌ DAISHI GYAKUSHU NIKKINOKOTO

It is not until we reach the Muromachi era that we find written sources referring to funerary rites and memorial services featuring the full Thirteen Buddhas. One of the oldest surviving documents I have uncovered in my research is the apocryphal scripture *Kōbō Daishi Gyakushu nikkinokoto* 弘法大師逆修日記事, believed to have first appeared sometime in the years intervening 1429-1441. This means that it would predate the *Kagakushū* 下学集[9], composed in 1444, another prominent source cited by scholars regarding the development of the Ten Kings into the Thirteen Buddhas. The *Kōbō Daishi Gyakushu nikkinokoto* lists the names of the Thirteen Buddhas with their individual Sanskrit seed syllables and a short description of their power or virtue. Like *The Scripture on Jizō and the Ten Kings*, the names of the Ten Kings are listed next to the first ten Buddhas. However, alongside the schedule of memorial observances, a fixed calendar date is also given for premortem worship listed as follows:

1. Fudō Myō-ō   16th day of the first month

2. Shaka Nyorai 29th day of the second month

3. Monju-bosatsu 25th day of the third month

4. Fugen-bosatsu 14th day of the fourth month

5. Jizō-bosatsu 24th day of the fifth month

6. Miroku-bosatsu 15th day of the sixth month

7. Yakushi Nyorai 8th day of the seventh month

8. Kannon-bosatsu 18th day of the eighth month

9. Seishi-bosatsu 23rd day of the ninth month

10. Amida Nyorai 15th day of the tenth month

11. Ashuku Nyorai 15th day of the eleventh month

12. Dainichi Nyorai 28th day of the eleventh month

13. Kokūzō bosatsu 13th day of the twelfth month

With regards to these specific premortem dates, it seems certain that they have been at least partially adopted from *The Secret Buddhist Deities of the Thirty days of the Month* (*sanjūnichi hibutsu* 三十日密仏).[10] This grouping of thirty Buddhist deities for separate days in the lunar month is most commonly attributed to Kai Zenshi 戒禅師, a tenth century Chinese monk who lived amidst the Zen monastic centers at Gosozan 五祖山 in the tenth century. Miyasaka notes that this custom of worshipping specific Buddhas on specific days was imported to Japan from China in the late Heian period and it spread widely throughout the country in the Kamakura era. I reproduce the list in table 5 below highlighting the members of the Thirteen Buddhas in bold (note: Fudō is the only deity who is not included).

1. Jōkō (定光)	2. Tōmyō (燈明)	3.Tahō (多宝)
4. **Ashuku**	5. **Miroku**	6. Nimantōmyō (二万燈明)
7. Sanmantōmyō (三萬燈明)	8. **Yakushi**	9. Daitsūchishō (大通智勝)
10. Nichigetsu Tōmyō (日月燈明)	11. Kangi (歓喜)	12. Nanshō (難勝)
13. **Kokūzō**	14. **Fugen**	15. **Amida**
16. Darani (陀羅尼)	17. Ryūju (龍樹)	18. **Kanzeon**
19. Nikkō (日光)	20. Gakkō (月光)	21. Mujini (無尽意)
22. Senmui (施無畏)	23. **Daiseishi** (大勢至)	24. **Jizō**
25. **Monju**	26. Yakujō (薬上)	27. Roshana (毘盧遮那)
28. **Dainichi**	29. Yaku-ō 薬王	30. **Shaka**

Table 5: The Secret Buddhist Deities of the Thirty days of the Month

If we compare the days given in the dates listed above with those recorded in the *Kōbō Daishi Gyakushu nikkinokoto*, we find that eight out of the twelve deities have matching days: Yakushi (8th), Kokūzō (13th), Fugen (14th) Amida (15th), Kanzeon (Kannon) (18th), Seishi (23rd), Jizō (24th), Monju (25th), Dainichi (28th). The equivalent days increase to nine if we compare the list with the *Kagakushū* (the date for Miroku is given as the fifth and not the fifteenth). The similarities in these days are too numerous to be considered just coincidental; and interestingly, they also correspond with another religious practice which emerged among members of the laity in the middle of the Heian era known as the *jūsainichi shinkō* 十斎日信仰. According to accounts given by Watanabe (1989) and Miyasaka (2011), practitioners of this belief designated ten days in a month to the worship of individual Buddhist deities known collectively as the *jūsainichibutsu* 十斎日仏. For these ten days, followers were instructed to obey the eight precepts (*hassaikai* 八斎戒): to abstain from killing, stealing, sexual activity, intoxicants, falsehood and so on. The dates chosen for each Buddhist deity are given as follows:

1st day   Jōkō

8th day Yakushi

14th day Fugen

15th day Amida

18th day Kannon

23rd day Seishi

24th day Jizō

28th day Dainichi

29th day Yaku-ō

30th day Shaka

As can be seen from the above list, eight of the ten *jūsainichibutsu* are also the *honjibutsu* of the Ten Kings as recorded in the *Kōbō Daishi*

Gyakushu nikkinokoto. What is particularly striking is that the days given for the Buddhas that appear in both lists match exactly— except for Shaka, who is listed as the twenty-ninth day in the *Kōbō Daishi Gyakushu nikkinokoto* (a difference of only one day). It is difficult to say how much of an influence this belief or the secret Buddhist deities of the 30 days of the month had on the development of the Thirteen Buddha Rites, but judging from the similarity in the days of worship, we can conclude that either, or both, had a pivotal influence in the establishment of the specific dates for premortem rituals.

As my summary of the main texts has shown, there are still many questions and inconsistencies that need to be resolved before we can draw any conclusions about the historical development of the Thirteen Buddha Rites. Part of the problem lies in the lack of any detailed exposition in these scriptures. *The Scripture on Jizō and the Ten Kings* shows us that the Buddhas were paired with the Chinese Ten Kings, but the relationship is purely normative; it doesn't explain the reasons why these particular Buddhas were assigned to the Ten Kings. The *Kōbō Daishi Gyakushu nikkinokoto,* clearly derives from The Scripture on the Ten Kings, but it says nothing about why three extra Buddhas were added or why the memorial service period was extended to thirty-three years. Finally, dates for premortem worship are allocated to each deity, but the scriptures fail to impart anything about the significance of these dates. Thus, due to the limited and fragmented nature of the written evidence available to researchers, anyone relying purely on such records alone faces a seemingly impossible task to explain the historical development of the Thirteen Buddha Rites without recourse to speculation. It is therefore necessary to take an alternative approach and interpret the numerological and symbolic correspondences contained within the Thirteen Buddha Rites to see if they reveal anything about their origin and deeper meanings. As we shall see in the next chapter, such an approach helps us to uncover some of the deepest historical roots of the Thirteen Buddha Rites.

Chapter Five

十三仏の密学
ESOTERIC INTERPRETATIONS

In order to find out the reasons why the number of Buddhist deities expanded to thirteen and the period of worship extended to thirty-three years, it is important to analyze these numbers from a numerological perspective and interpret their hidden meanings. With regards to the number thirty-three, we find an interesting correlation with the thirty-three transformational bodies of Kannon. According to the Lotus Sūtra, Kannon changes into the most suitable of thirty-three different forms to save those in distress. These forms are varied and range from a military general to a wife, child or local god. Corresponding to these thirty-three forms, pilgrimage routes to thirty-three temples, the oldest dating from the Heian Period, spread throughout Japan and remain popular to this day.

If we look outside the Buddhist tradition and consider indigenous beliefs and customs associated with ancestor worship, we find that thirty-three years also marks the point in time when the deceased's spirit passes from 'distant' to 'remote' and they become a fully-fledged ancestor of the household. In this sense, the number thirty-three signifies a juncture of ascension and this explains why it would have been desirable to extend the memorial dates to thirty-three years in the Thirteen Buddha Rites.[11]

The reason as to why the number of Buddhist deities extended to thirteen became a subject of investigation for the influential folklore scholar Yanagita Kunio (1875-1962). He became interested in the links between the *jūsanbutsu* and the phenomenon of *jūsantzuka* 十三塚 (groups of thirteen memorial mounds) discovered across Japan; and in his written correspondence, a host of theories are speculated regarding the significance of the number thirteen. The most interesting of these include one which divides the number into twelve plus one to mimic the sun passing through the twelve months of the year (or signs of the zodiac). When looked at from this perspective, the cycle of time leading from death to rebirth in the Thirteen Buddha Rites mimic or embody the annual seasonal changes—from the moribund months of autumn to the rejuvenation of spring.

It is also possible to connect each of the thirteen deities with the thirteen months of the lunar year. As Japan adopted its astrological practices from China, following the lunar calendar, this would seem to be a more valid argument. Certainly, there are other Japanese Buddhist traditions explicitly linked to the Chinese Zodiac which could be informative. The Twelve Heavenly Generals (*jūnishinshō* 十二神将) who guard Yakushi Nyorai are such an example. Originally Hindu Yaksha deities, they were first introduced to Japan as protective warriors in the 6th and 7th century AD. They later became associated with the twelve daylight hours and twelve months of the year and were said to regulate agricultural cycles. Statues of the Generals are often displayed forming a protective circle around Yakushi who embodies the *axis mundi* flanked either side by Nikkō and Gakkō (Bodhisattvas of the Sun and moon). During the Heian period, the Twelve Heavenly Generals became connected to the twelve animals of the Chinese Zodiac, and sculptures, such as those on display at Kannami Buddha statues Museum in Shizuoka prefecture, began to show the signs of the Zodiac carved into their headdress. In the village of Nozawa Onsen in Nagano prefecture, individual statues of the Twelve Heavenly Generals and a Yakushi triad are housed inside thirteen separate communal hot springs known as *sotoyu* 外湯. Tourists who embark on the *sotoyu meguri* (hot spring pilgrimage) to bathe in each of the thirteen hot springs do so unaware that the ritual derives from the waxing and waning of the moon in a lunar calendar year.

Like the Ten Kings of Hell, the Twelve Heavenly Generals were also assimilated into the *Honji suijaku* paradigm where they were seen as manifestations of original Buddhist deities *(honjibutsu)*. Although the assigned *honjibutsu* and the Japanese names of the 12 Heavenly Generals are not always consistent, a common designation reads as follows:

Heavenly General	Honjibutsu
Bikara Taishō	Shaka
Shotora Taishō	Dainichi
Shindara Taishō	Fugen
Makora Taishō	Daitoku Myō-ō
Haira Taishō	Monju
Indara Taishō	Jizō
Sanchira Taishō	Kokūzō
Ajira Taishō	Nyoirin Kannon
Anchira Taishō	Kannon Bosatsu
Mekira Taishō	Amida
Basara Taishō	Seishi
Kubira Taishō	Miroku

Table 6: The Twelve Heavenly Generals and their Honjibutsu

If we add Yakushi to this list and compare it with the Thirteen Buddhas, the presence of Daitoku Myō-ō and the esoteric Nyoirin Kannon instead of Fudō Myō-ō and Ashuku are the only differences.

Concerning esoteric interpretations of the Thirteen Buddha Rites, James Sanford uncovered a Shingon affiliated text called the *Sangai isshinki* 三界一心記 which connects the Thirteen Buddhas with the embryonic stages of fetal development.

From Sanford's translation:

> Originally there was a single seed of brightness that divided and became the six conjunctions. This is also called the twin red and white drops of mother and father. These congeal to form a five-colored letter *a*. Menstrual flow ceases and on the first seventh-day [the embryo] takes on the shape of a jellyfish. [...] On the first seventh-day Fudō Myō-ō 不動明王 is taken as the *honzon*. The character *fu* 不 consists of "one" 一 over "small" 小 and *dō* 動 is "power" 力 "made heavy" 重. Myō 明, "bright," is man and woman (since it is composed of "sun" 日 and "moon" 月), while the three horizontal strokes of *ō* 王, "king," are father, mother and child.
>
> [...] In the second month the embryo in the mother's womb takes the shape of a wishing-jewel finial on a monk's staff. During the second seven days, Shaka is made the *honzon*. The characters of his name, 釋迦 (in premodern orthography) have as their constituents "rice" 米 and "to soak" 睪, "added together" 加 and stirred around 辶. In the mother's womb something like a sizing paste of milk and powdered rice begins to develop and the mother begins to make milk. Within the womb, the child is nestled down. It still has the form of a priest's staff". (See Sanford, 1997, p.28)

The text continues in this manner assigning Buddhas to specific developmental stages of the child in the womb. The numerical problems of matching ten months of pregnancy with thirteen deities is overcome by extending the stages of fetal Buddhahood into the fully developed adulthood of the new body. Thus, in the *Sangai isshinki* these thirteen stages lead beyond death and rebirth, to enlightenment marked by a return to the Womb of Emptiness (Kokūzō).

The inclusion of Kokūzō is another fascinating element in the development of the Thirteen Buddha Rites. Although prominent in the Shingon sect as the deity of the *gumonjihō* meditation ritual, Kenji Sano's study on Kokūzō worship shows how he has also been the center of a rich history of folk beliefs and rituals including mountain ascetic practices (*shugendō* 修験道). Taking this into account, it is certainly plausible that his addition might have just naturally evolved from his popularity during the early Heian period. This is the argument purported by some Japanese scholars, most notably Kawakatsu. Nonetheless, it is important to note that Kokūzō (womb of emptiness) exists in juxtaposition with his counterpart Jizō (womb of the earth), and when their relationship is viewed within the context of the Thirteen Buddha Rites, Jizō leads the spirit out of hell (*jigoku* 地獄) and Kokūzō guides it towards paradise (*gokuraku* 極楽). In more esoteric terms, his place as the thirteenth and final Buddha, can be seen to mark the final stage in the transmutation of matter to ether.

PART TWO

十三仏石造資料

ARCHAEOLOGICAL EVIDENCE OF THE THIRTEEN BUDDHA RITES

The Thirteen Buddhas

Stone stele from *Dainenji in Nara,* dated 1555.

INTRODUCTION

Before investigating further, it may be useful to briefly summarize the chronology of the written records examined in part one. Through the early records in *kanbun nikki* such as the *Chūyūki,* we have seen that memorial services and seven seventh-day premortem rites connected to Buddhist deities on specific dates were carried out in Japan as far back as the 12th century by members of the ruling dynasty. However, it is not until the early 15th century that written records such as the *Kōbō Daishi Gyakushu nikkinokoto* and the *Kagakushū* show the Thirteen Buddha series of rites in their currently accepted order. It is therefore the period of time between the late Kamakura and early Muromachi eras that deserves the closest attention if we are to uncover the origin of the Thirteen Buddha Rites. I have already touched on how the Chinese belief in the Ten Kings started to spread through Japan during this period, culminating in *The Scripture on Jizō and the Ten Kings*— believed to be the template for what would later become the Thirteen Buddha Rites. However, the argument that three extra Buddhas were then added to the *honjibutsu* of the Ten Kings sometime during the Muromachi era oversimplifies a more complex development revealed to us by a close examination of surviving Buddhist monuments and stone steles, known as *itabi* 板碑. In this chapter, I shall discuss some of the most significant archaeological findings and discuss what they can tell us about the historical development of the Thirteen Buddha Rites.

The Thirteen Buddhas

Stone stele from *Hōzenji* temple dated 1664.

Chapter Six

保月六面石幢
HOTSUKI ROKUMENSEKIDŌ

Watanabe estimates that there are more than four hundred surviving memorials and monuments (*ihin* 遺品) relating to the Thirteen Buddhas across Japan (1989, p.210). One of the earliest and most impressive discovered so far is a six-sided stone pillar known as the *Hotsuki Rokumensekidō* 保月六面石幢 located in the outskirts of Hosooji 臍帯寺 in Okayama prefecture (see Fig 1.1). A total of twelve Buddhas can be seen carved into the six sides of the pillar which measures just over two and a half meters in height and is dated 1306. One side of the pillar has a group of seven deities carved into the face of the stone, headed by Miroku, and descending in pairs from top to bottom, left to right: Yakushi/Shaka, Jizō/ Monju, Fudō/ Fugen (see fig 1.1/1.2). Five other deities - Kannon, Seishi, Amida, Kokūzō and a variation of Fudō seated on a lotus flower instead of a rock - are carved individually on the five remaining sides.

The Thirteen Buddhas

Fig 1.1   Fig 1.2

Hotsuki Rokumensekidō,
Okayama prefecture, H.265 cm, dated 1306.

Sanskrit seed syllables are engraved below the five deities occupying the five separate sides of the pillar. However, it is the written words in Japanese below the group of Buddhas that are of particular interest, which read as follows:

「…初七日至十三年相当□彫刻仏菩薩十二尊像為証大菩提」

(Twelve Buddhist deities for the first seven days to the thirteenth year)

The inscription shows that the pillar was constructed for rituals

75

connected to twelve Buddhist deities, and Kawakatsu alleges that it was likely used for premortem offerings as opposed to memorial services for the deceased. But what else can be surmised from this monument? Yajima asserts that the connection of the Buddhas with the period of time extending to thirteen years reveals an intermediate stage of development between the Ten Kings and the Thirteen Buddhas. In other words, this pillar indicates a 'transitional period' where the selection of Buddhist deities started to exceed beyond ten, but had not yet reached the fixed order of what would later become the Thirteen Buddhas. As the pillar was constructed after the belief in the Ten Kings entered Japan, but predates the earliest written records of the Thirteen Buddha Rites, this seems distinctly possible. Nonetheless, it remains somewhat problematic to connect this selection of Buddhist deities directly to the Thirteen Buddha Rites without overlooking the anomaly of the appearance of two separate Fudōs. Whilst other monuments from around this period show similar variations in the selection of Buddhas, I have not discovered any in my research that feature two Fudōs. As noted earlier, Fudō was the only member of the Thirteen Buddhas not included in the secret Buddhist deities of the 30 days of the month, so his twofold presence here would at least seem to discount any association of this monument with that particular custom. Fudō aside, Dainichi and Ashuku are the only other absent members of the Thirteen Buddhas. They would both start to be included together in their accepted positions (eleventh and twelfth) in monuments and memorials constructed at the beginning of the fifteenth century, as I demonstrate later.

The Thirteen Buddhas

Chapter Seven

延命寺十二尊種子曼荼羅
ENMEIJI JŪNISON SHUJI MANDALA

Another example that further illustrates this transitional period is a stone memorial monument located in a Shingon temple in Yamagata prefecture called Enmeiji 延命寺. Somewhat similar in size and appearance to a cemetery headstone, it is known as the *jūnison shuji mandara* 十二尊種子曼荼羅 (see Fig 1.3 opposite).

Fig.1.3 *jūnison shuji mandara,* Yamagata prefecture, Enmeiji.
H.85 cm, W.85cm, diameter of outer circle disk 59 cm, dated 1359.

As its name suggests, it depicts twelve Buddhas in their Sanskrit seed syllable format. A large circular moon disk (*gachirin* 月輪) is engraved on the face of the stone containing a smaller circle inside it which houses the Sanskrit seed syllables of the Amida triad (Amida, Seishi, Kannon). The Amida triad is often featured in memorials and steles dating from the Kamakura and Muromachi era independent from any belief in the Ten Kings/Thirteen Buddhas.[12] However, in this case, the Sanskrit letters of nine Buddhas encircle the Amida triad in the center circle like the numbers around the face of a clock. The names of the nine Buddhas, starting from the top, are given as follows in clockwise order: Fudō, Shaka, Monju, Fugen, Jizō, Miroku, Yakushi, Ashuku, Kongō Satta. The inclusion of twelve deities suggest a movement towards the

Thirteen Buddhas, but the centrality of the Amida triad in this monument indicate that this could also be looked on as Ten Buddhas with Amida as the main *honzon* (The Amida triad counting as one single Buddha). The appearance of Kongō Satta provides another problem for researchers attempting to link this monument with the Thirteen Buddha Rites. Kawakatsu says that although the addition of Ashuku is consistent with a general transition towards the Thirteen Buddhas, he is at a loss to explain why Kongō should be included. One possibility is that the Sanskrit inscription for Kongō Satta could have been mistakenly transmitted instead of Dainichi's. There are at least four different Sanskrit syllables that can be used to represent the various incarnations of Dainichi (see Fig 1.4), and there are cases, especially within the Shingon and Tendai sects, where there are alternative *shuji* for the same *honzon*. The levels of esoteric knowledge required to understand their full meaning is sizeable, and the oral tradition (*kuden* 口伝) through which such knowledge was passed on means that it is certainly possible that the *shuji* for Dainichi was somehow mistranslated. Watanabe asserts, however, that the inclusion of Kongō Satta is characteristic of a regional variation attributed to folk religious beliefs. According to Watanabe, such traditions commonly fused aspects of Amida and Jizō cults and a range of disparate religious practices to form their own combinatory form of religions that were particularly prevalent in rural towns and villages such as this.

Dainichi Womb Realm *"āḥ"* (アーク)

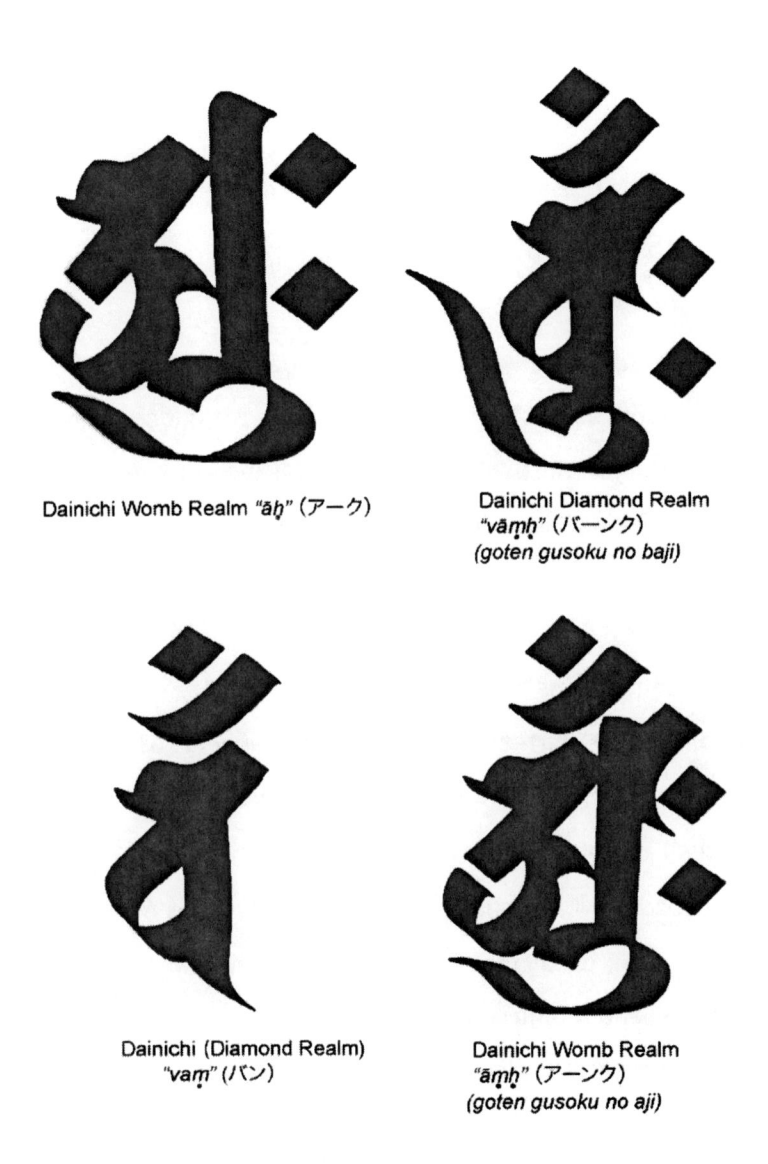

Dainichi Diamond Realm *"vāṃḥ"* (バーンク)
(goten gusoku no baji)

Dainichi (Diamond Realm) *"vaṃ"* (バン)

Dainichi Womb Realm *"āṃḥ"* (アーンク)
(goten gusoku no aji)

Fig 1.4 Sanskrit Seed syllables (*shuji*) for Dainichi Nyorai

Chapter Eight

慈光寺十三仏種子板碑
JIKŌJI JŪSANBUTSU SHUJI ITABI

A stone stele dated slighted earlier (1345) can perhaps be connected to the Thirteen Buddha Rites with far less contention. It is located in Saitama prefecture, just north of Tokyo, in the precincts of a temple called *Jikōji* 慈光寺 which is affiliated with the Tendai sect. Scholars are in agreement that if the engraved date is accurate, this is the oldest *itabi* so far discovered to feature thirteen Buddhas; although, three of those are different versions of Dainichi so technically it has to be differentiated from the Thirteen Buddhas. Dainichi appears as the *honzon* for the seventh, thirteenth and thirty-third years, manifesting in the Sanskrit seed syllables of both his Womb (*taizōkai* 胎蔵界) and Diamond (*kongōkai* 金剛界) realms. The other ten Buddhas mostly follow the same order used in the Thirteen Buddha Rites, except for the positions of Fugen and Monju who have swapped their places at third and fourth respectively (see picture opposite). Incongruities such as this are difficult to fathom, but as the Shaka triad of Shaka, Monju and Fugen remains in order, the interchange of positions between the latter two can perhaps be overlooked as a minor anomaly.

The particular style of calligraphy used to engrave the Sanskrit on this *itabi* and others from this period, is known as *yagenbori* 薬研彫. This technique, which involves carving the grooves of the characters in a V-shape, is thought to have become established around the Muromachi period, and it was often used to engrave stone monuments and even Buddhist stupas.

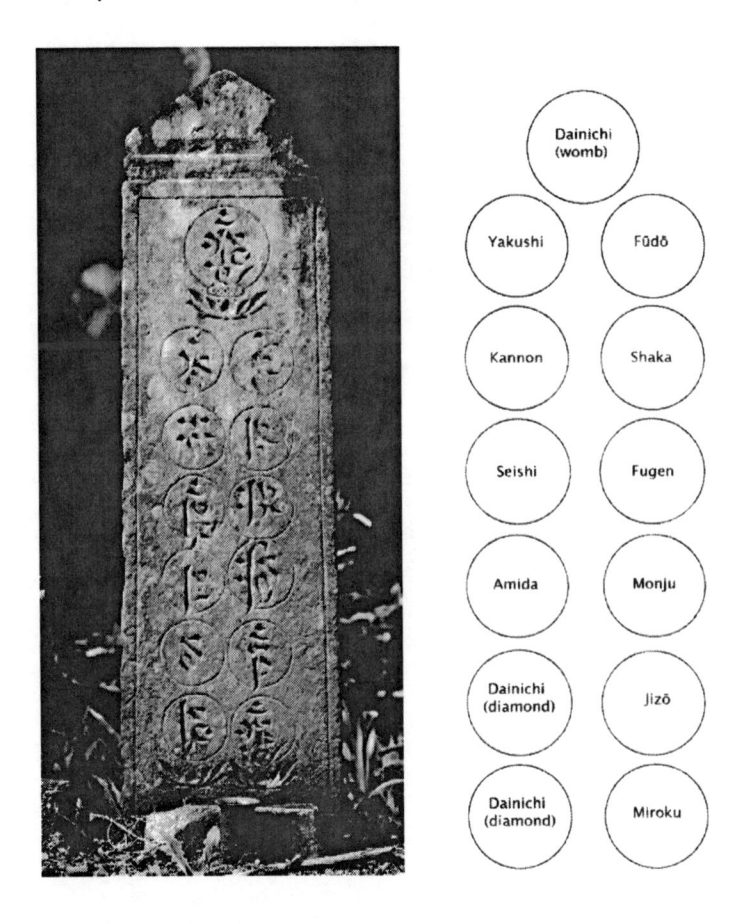

Saitama prefecture, Jikōji, *jūsanbutsu shuji itabi*.
H.140cm, W.45cm, dated 1345.

The Sanskrit seed syllable placed at the top of the tablet is a character uniquely used in Japan to represent the womb realm of Dainichi. It is known as the *goten gusoku no aji* 五点具足のア字, pronounced āmh

(アーンク). This combines with the *kongōkai goten gusoku no baji* 金剛界五点具足のバ字 pronounced vāmh (バーンク) placed in the twelfth position (bottom left side), and the more orthodox *shuji* of the diamond realm (*vam*) above it to create a Dainichi trinity. Sano records the eleventh character to stand for Ashuku (1996, p.117) but that seems unlikely when we compare it with other monuments from this period, as they also seem to feature Dainichi as the last three Buddhas (see page 91). The Buddhas line up in two vertical rows crowned by Dainichi at the top. It is worth pointing out that the research of Kataoka Nagaharu has revealed that the pattern of the Buddhas on these monuments varies quite considerably, especially between the Kansai and Kantō regions. Most monuments feature the Buddhas arranged in one of the following four patterns: two columns of six; three columns of four; Buddhas centered around the Amida triad, and individual stone Buddhas. Two vertical columns of six Buddhas crowned with the thirteenth Buddha seems to be the most common pattern, particularly in the Kansai region. His work is a telling reminder that geographical location should also be factored into the equation if we are to better understand the differences that arise between these monuments throughout Japan.

The Thirteen Buddhas

Chapter Nine

羽黒十三仏堂板碑
HAGURO JŪSANBUTSUDŌ ITABI

A similar monument dated slightly later (1378) can be observed in Haguro, Chiba prefecture. This stone *itabi* is housed inside a small, shrine-like construction known as the *Haguro jūsanbutsudō* 羽黒十三仏堂. Although the engravings have faded with time, scholars have been able to decipher the Sanskrit letters as the *honjibutsu* of the Ten Kings and three separate seed syllables of Dainichi: *a, vam, āmh*. Kawakatsu asserts that it was likely used by a community of lay religious practitioners for premortem rituals. He also remarks that elderly women from the village continue to gather in the *butsudō* on the evening of the fourteenth of each month, most likely to greet the dawn of Amida's day (recorded as the fifteenth day in the secret Buddhist deities of the 30 days of the month). If true, it is possible that the origin of the monument could owe more to beliefs and rituals related to Amida than Thirteen Buddha Rites.

Haguro *jūsanbutsudō itabi,* Chiba Prefecture.
H.117cm, W.97cm, dated 1378.

Chapter Ten

深谷十三仏群
FUKATANI JŪSANBUTSUGUN

The earliest archaeological find I have discovered so far that shows a collection of deities explicitly connected to the Thirteen Buddha Rites is located in the town of Tokuji in Yamaguchi prefecture. Thirteen Buddhist deities have been carved into individual stone statues, seven of which have been housed inside a small pavilion. The remaining six statues are placed outside the building (see fig 1.7) and they are all approximately 70 cm in height. Access to the site remains unrestricted; and the size and layout of the building suggests that it was likely a place for communal worship as well as a destination for religious pilgrimages. Unfortunately, archaeologists have not been able to clearly identify any of the Buddha's from the worn out engravings, bar one, Kokūzō, who is placed in the center. The engraving on the back of the Kokūzō statue reads as follows:

The Thirteen Buddhas

Fig 1.7 *Fukatani jūsanbutsugun*,
Yamaguchi prefecture, Tokuji, dated 1407.

Fig 1.8

```
       応
       永
       十
       四
       丁
   修 刻 逆
       二
       月
       彼
       岩
```

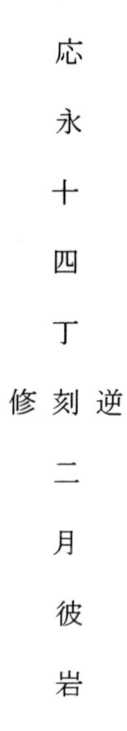

The Chinese characters aligned vertically merely confirm the date of the structure as being built in 1407, but the characters that intersect horizontally read as "*gyakushu*", denoting that the stone Buddhas were built explicitly for the purpose of premortem rituals. This provides irrefutable archaeological evidence of the existence of Thirteen Buddha Rites as far back as 1407, making this date a key moment in their historical development. In order to give an overview of the progression of the final three Buddhas in similar monuments from this period, I have placed it in the following chronological chart, adapted from the studies of Watanabe and Sano.

The Thirteen Buddhas

Date	Location	Final Three Buddhas
1345	Saitama, Jikōji	Dainichi, Dainichi, Dainichi
1378	Chiba, Haguro	Dainichi, Dainichi, Dainichi
1386	Chiba, Sahara, Jōdoji	Dainichi, Dainichi, Dainichi
1399	Tokyo, Nakano, Seikokuji	Dainichi, Dainichi, Dainichi
1407	**Yamaguchi, Tokuji**	**Ashuku, Dainichi, Kokūzō**
1413	Hyōgo, Kanzaki-gun	Ashuku, Dainichi, Dainichi
1414	Ōita, Bungatakadashi	Ashuku, Dainichi, Kokūzō
1442	Saitama, Tōkōin	Dainichi, Dainichi, Kokūzō
1447	**Tokyo, Minamitama-gun**	**Ashuku, Dainichi, Kokūzō**
1474	**Gunma, Gunma-gun**	**Ashuku, Dainichi, Kokūzō**
1479	**Nara, Shigisan**	**Ashuku, Dainichi, Kokūzō**

Although this is not a comprehensive list that covers all the monuments, it does provide enough evidence to assert that the transitional period between the Ten Kings and the Thirteen Buddha Rites lasted for at least a century. We can see that from the earliest monument discovered in 1345, up to a period beginning in 1407, Dainichi was mainly incorporated alongside the *honjibutsu* of the Ten Kings. After that we start to see the addition of Ashuku and Kokūzō with some minor rearrangements, before the monuments begin to settle into the established Thirteen Buddha Rites order in the second half of the fifteenth century. This latter development owes much to the appearance of the earliest written documents, such as the *Kagakushū* (1444), which laid a template for the Thirteen Buddha Rites; but how are we to explain the existence of Thirteen Buddha memorial sites found decades before such as the *Fukatani jūsanbutsugun*? Further, what can monuments such as the *Hotsuki Rokumensekidō,* which appeared at least a hundred years before the first written documents, tell us about the origin of the Thirteen Buddha Rites? I shall attempt to answer these questions and point to other areas which need further study in the following conclusion.

The Thirteen Buddhas

結論
CONCLUSION

In the written documents discussed in chapter one, I confirmed that postmortem offerings and rituals conducted by the elite members of Japanese society were carried out as far back as the eighth century. From the court records of the twelfth century onwards, we then find seven seventh-day rites associated with various Buddhist deities for both postmortem, and premortem rituals.

The art, literature and rituals pertaining to the Ten Kings of Hell began to spread amongst the Japanese general populace in the early thirteenth century and Jizō's identification as the alter ego of Enma ō made him an essential element in the implementation of the *honji suijaku* paradigm made explicit in *The Scripture on Jizō and the Ten Kings*. This belief took hold and developed during the Kamakura period at a time when other beliefs and traditions such as the *sanjūnichi hibutsu* and the *jūsainichi shinkō* were worshipping Buddhist deities on specific dates. The Japanese secondary sources I referenced are very vague on the details of these practices but, nonetheless, we can conclude that they had a strong influence on the days of the month recorded for premortem worship in the *Kōbō Daishi Gyakushu nikkinokoto*. This apocryphal scripture, one of the earliest written records of the Thirteen Buddha Rites, emerged in the early Muromachi era, and legitimized the Thirteen Buddha Rites as a Shingon religious practice. Today it remains most commonly affiliated with the Shingon sect, but I have demonstrated how its roots run deep across a variety of both postmortem and premortem rituals.

The archaeological evidence that I brought to light in part two shows how some of the surviving monuments predate the earliest written records. The most striking example is the *Fukatani jūsanbutsugun*, which, if the 1407 date is accurate, is the earliest record of the Thirteen Buddha Rites so far discovered in both written and archaeological evidence. There are, as I have shown, stone steles and memorial sites which are dated even earlier, but the selection and arrangement of the deities are not systematic, and therefore it is difficult to connect them directly to the Thirteen Buddha Rites. Japanese researchers are prone to use the generic terms "*shominshinkō*" 庶民信仰 or "*minkan shinkō*" 民間信仰 (folk religious beliefs) to explain the presence of two Fudō's on the *Hotsuki Rokumensekidō* or the inclusion of Kongō Satta on the *Enmeiji jūnison shuji mandara*; but without clarifying precisely who these folk religious communities were and what they believed, this is not a satisfactory explanation and I suggest more research here is required. We must also remain open to the possibilities that more extensive field research could uncover other sites and monuments that would predate the ones I have discussed here. In the same manner, more investigation into courtier diaries and other written documents might reveal evidence that redefines the chronology of the Thirteen Buddha Rites I have outlined here.

Recent studies have given us a greater understanding of the historical roots of the Thirteen Buddha Rites, but many unanswered questions still remain about their precise origin which need to be looked into. The *honji suijaku* paradigm has been used to usurp or incorporate antecedent traditions into Buddhist ritual practice, and we have seen how the Thirteen Buddha Rites are no different in this regard. The question then arises, can the rites be traced back even further past earlier Buddhist, Hindu and Taoist customs? The answer is hidden in plain sight with the conscious use of the sacred mystical numbers seven and thirteen. The emphasis on the number seven can only derive from the Seven Planets of the Ancients (The Sun and Moon, Mercury, Venus, Mars Jupiter and Saturn) from which we get our days of the week. Thirteen, as we have seen, designates the thirteen moon cycles in a year, or the sun passing through the twelve signs of the zodiac. Either way, it suggests that the deepest roots of the Thirteen Buddha Rites stem from an ancient form of astrotheology—a theology founded on the observation of the heavenly bodies. Thus, ultimately, the deceased's journey from death to reincarnation in the Thirteen Buddha Rites, embody the grander motions and cycles of sidereal time, unifying the microcosm of the individual with the macrocosm of the universe.

The Thirteen Buddhas

あとがき

THIRTEEN BUDDHA PILGRIMAGE IN YAMAGATA

The Thirteen Buddha pilgrimage in Yamagata prefecture started in 1992 and incorporates some very interesting temples across the Shingon, Tendai, Pure Land and Soto Zen Buddhist sects. Each temple features a *honzon* of one of the thirteen deities, which is usually housed inside a separate building from the main temple. Some of the temples are also part of one of several thirty-three temple Kannon pilgrimages operating in the same area, so visitors and tourists are expected. However, to avoid disappointment, it is best to contact the temples in advance and let them know when you are coming to be sure you can gain access to the *honzon*.

Navigating the local bus and train routes to each temple can be quite challenging and some advance planning is definitely recommended. I managed to make my way to most of the sites on foot from the nearest train station, but trains and buses are infrequent and can sometimes keep you waiting for two hours or more. You should be prepared to expect to stay for at least a couple of days to have enough time to visit all the temples.

Each temple usually has a small reception area for visitors, and the priest or a family member will be happy to take you to the *honzon* and answer any questions about the history of the temple. You will be given privacy to pray, chant and light incense candles if you desire. You can also purchase a small notebook as a memento that the priests of each temple will stamp and adorn with calligraphy for 300 yen. Photography inside the temples is sometimes prohibited so it is courteous to ask for permission before taking any photographs.

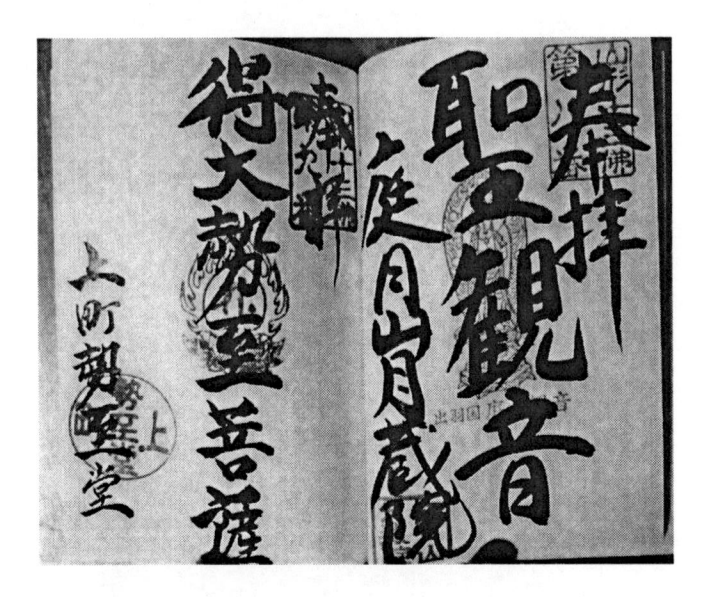

A photo of the inside of the 13 Buddha notebook stamped with the names of Kannon on the right and Seishi on the left.

Recommended Route

It is not necessary to visit the temples in any particular order so you can plan a route which is most convenient for you. Yamagata station is a good base to start from and gives you access to the main train lines and bus routes across Yamagata prefecture. I used the following route from south to north:

13 Kokūzō ➡12 Dainichi ➡1 Fudō ➡9 Seishi ➡11 Ashuku ➡7 Yakushi ➡10 Amida ➡6 Miroku ➡3 Monjū ➡13 Kokūzō ➡2 Shaka ➡5 Jizō ➡4 Fugen ➡8 Kannon

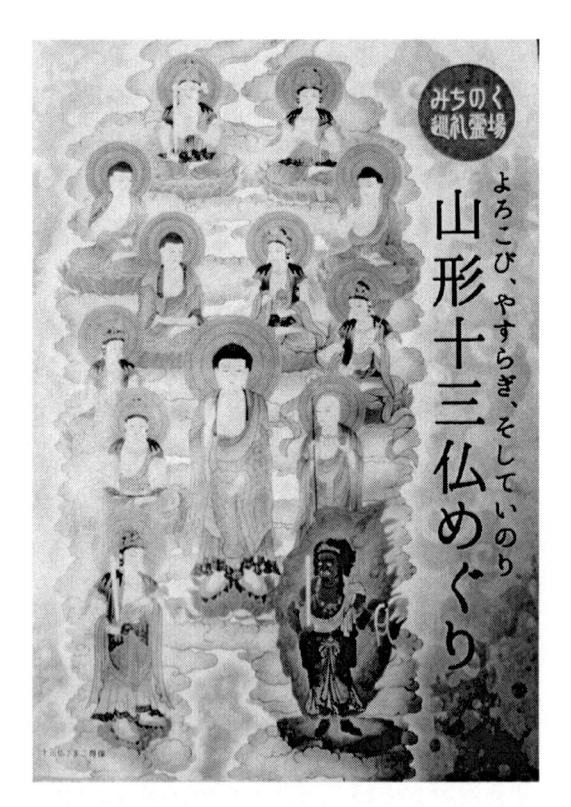

A promotional pamphlet for the 13 Buddha Pilgrimage in Yamagata prefecture.

Sōfukuin (宗福院)　　Sect: Tendai　　Honzon: Fudō Myō-ō

Sōfukuin is one of four temples within comfortable walking distance of Yamagata station. The temple is about thirty minutes walk south from the station and is located close to a grandiose Nichiren temple. The temple is said to have been built in 708 AD and is host to a pleasant rock garden which features a Kannon water fountain in the middle. As a designated site for three separate Kannon pilgrimages, tourists visit here to drink the fountain's purifying water and pay their respects to the Bodhisattva of mercy. Sōfukuin is also the twelfth temple of an eighty-eight-temple pilgrimage also operating in Yamagata prefecture. In the rear of the temple grounds you will find a stone statue of Fudō placed on top of a rock in a sand garden. The main *honzon* is housed inside the adjacent building and depicts a fierce looking Fudō surrounded by red flames holding his sword and binding rope.

Jōsenji (乗船寺)　　Sect: Pure Land　　Honzon: Shaka

Located in the center of Yamagata prefecture, ten minutes on foot from Ōishita station, Jōsenji houses a wooden statue of Shaka in the nirvana pose—lying on his side. The two meter long, gold painted statue was constructed in the Edo period and installed here in 1694. Shaka appears to be peacefully resting with his eyes closed and his head gently supported by his right hand. Statues of the Buddha in this pose are very rare, and people reportedly travel from all over Japan to see it.

Jōsenji is also host to a statue of a thousand-armed Kannon and a seated Amida— both protected as national treasures. The statues are expertly carved from wood and have been beautifully preserved. The Kannon is 45 cm tall and dated 1333, the seated Amida is 36 cm tall and is said to have been made during the late Heian period.

Ryugenji (龍源寺)　Sect: Sōtō-Zen　Honzon: Shaka triad (Monjū)

This temple is located high in the mountains of the Tenjō district and takes about ninety minutes on foot from Tenjō station. The temple itself is very austere, as is conventional in the Sōtō Zen tradition. The Sōtō Zen sect itself is comparatively quite strong in Yamagata prefecture, and six of the thirteen temples are Sōtō affiliated.

Inside the main hall, Monjū is displayed as part of the Shaka triad. He can be seen on the right side of Shaka riding on top of a lion. Zen disciples pay homage to Monjū so they can be given the fortitude to persevere through the physically and mentally demanding Zazen meditation practices. Monjū is also a popular deity with students who come to pay homage to him so they may be blessed with his wisdom and pass their exams.

Shōgenji (正源寺) Sect: Sōtō -Zen   Honzon: Shaka triad (Fugen)

Shōgenji is situated in the town of Mamurogawa in the most northern part of Yamagata prefecture. The temple is a short fifteen-minute walk from Mamurogawa station and is located right beside the railway tracks. It was built in 1535 and houses a Shaka triad of which Fugen assumes his position on the left side, riding on top of an elephant.

There is a pilgrimage to 108 Jizō sites in Yamagata prefecture of which Shōgenji is listed as temple 102. Consequently, in the entrance yard to the temple you can see a large statue of Jizō as well as a group of six small Jizo's adorned in red caps and bibs. Further back, there is an entrance way protected by two fierce looking guardians known as *Niō* (仁王). These are believed to protect the temple against evil spirits. One has its mouth open and the other its mouth closed representing life and death.

Kenshōji (見性寺)   Sect: Sōtō-Zen   Honzon: Jizō

Kenshōji is located in the north-western side of Yamagata along the Ogunigawa river which flows all the way to the North Pacific Ocean. The closest train station is Mogami, which is about an hours ride east from Shinjo on the Riku uto line. The temple is a fifteen-minute walk from the station.

There is a sizeable graveyard in the temple grounds containing some nicely carved stone statues of Amida and Kannon. Opposite the graveyard you will find a large stone statue of Jizō surrounded by a collection of smaller Jizō statues. The *honzon* is housed inside a separate wooden construction outside of the main temple. The residents told me that the healing powers of this Jizō are celebrated and the priest's wife testified to its miraculous curing qualities.

Mirokuin（弥勒院）　Sect: Shingon　Honzon: Miroku

   Mirokuin is located close to Kahoku hospital which is commutable by bus from Moriyama station. Out of the thirteen sites, it is the only Shingon affiliated temple; somewhat surprising considering the Thirteen Buddha Rites are commonly viewed to be a Shingon custom. Unlike the Sōtō-Zen temples, Mirokuin is colorful and lavishly decorated with pictures, statues and gold painted ornaments. The dramatic change in aesthetic is quite striking, and the temple feels vibrant and full of life. A bronze statue of Miroku is placed above Dainichi in the central display surrounded by various food offerings and candles. To the left you can find another statue of Miroku which is a replica of the famous Chūgūji sculpture. To the right you can see a statue of Kūkai, the founder of Shingon Buddhism, holding a three-pronged vajra. A painting of the Womb World Mandala hangs above the entrance.

Eirinji (永林寺)   Sect: Sōtō-Zen   Honzon: Yakushi

Eirinji was built sometime in the 14th century. It is located in the town of Asahi in the southwest of Yamagata and is unfortunately quite difficult to access by public transport. The closest train station is Aterazawa, and from there you need to catch a bus into Asahi town.

The main hall of the temple features a rather unusual Shaka triad with Kokūzō on the left and Amida stood on the right side. Yakushi is hidden behind Shaka as a *hibutsu* (a secret Buddha not shown to the public). The practice of maintaining *hibutsu* seems to have developed sometime during the Heian period. The head priest usually decides when they may be shown, and public viewings (known as *kaichō* 開帳) can be seasonal, annual or in cycles of seven, thirty-three or sixty years.

Gatsuzōin (月蔵院)　Sect: Tendai　Honzon: Kannon

Gatsuzōin, more commonly known as Niwatsuki temple, is located in the north of Yamagata prefecture about an hour on foot from Mamurogawa station. It has a rich history dating back to the Heian period and is probably the most illustrious temple of the thirteen. Gatsuzōin is the final site of a thirty-three-temple Kannon pilgrimage that dates back over 600 years. Kannon devotees come from all over Japan to pay their respects to the Bodhisattva of mercy. A special event is held every year on August 18th (Kannon's holy day) when the Sakegawa river, which flows nearby the temple precinct, is illuminated with thousands of floating candles.

The *honzon* is housed inside a wooden hut on the outskirts of the temple. It was constructed in 1676. Kannon stands in front of a mirror holding a lotus flower in his left hand. His right hand is held in front of his chest with the thumb and index finger pressed together, similar to the welcoming mudra used by Amida.

Seishidō (勢至堂)   Sect: Unaffiliated   Honzon: Seishi

The Seishidō is a fifteen-minute walk from Yamagata station and is perhaps the most curious temple out of the thirteen. Originally a Shingon temple built in 1671, it was gradually run down and abandoned. However, it was reconstructed in 1910 with donations from the local community and became a religious site unaffiliated with any Buddhist sect. The temple is currently looked after and maintained by members of local voluntary committees and organizations.

The entrance to the temple features an intriguing collection of thirteen stone Buddha statues, some of which are shown in their tantric (multi-armed) form. The temple itself is very small and consists of a modest display in the main hall with an Amida triad on the right, and a statue of Fudō on the left. A 568cm tall, wood-carved statue of Seishi takes center stage, standing with his hands pressed together in the "praying hands" pose.

Seiganji (誓願寺)   Sect: Pure Land   Honzon: Amida

Seiganji, the tenth temple of the pilgrimage, is a little difficult to access by public transport. The closest train station is Aterazawa. From there, follow route 458 north towards Sagae-gawa river, you will find the temple just off of route 112. Seiganji was originally built around two hundred years ago but since then it has twice been badly damaged by fire. It was reconstructed quite recently, in 1988, and evokes the style of a temple from the mid-Edo period.

Inside the main hall, a stone statue of Amida takes center place with his right hand held up in the "fear not" mudra. This version of Amida was based on the famous Amida triad from Zenkoji temple in Nagano, one of the first Buddhist images ever brought to Japan. To the left of the *honzon* there is a display of thirty-three small golden statues of Amida aligned in three rows of eleven.

Tenjōji (天性寺)　　Sect: Sōtō-Zen　　Honzon: Ashuku

Tenjōji is located about fifteen minutes on foot from Uzen Nagasaki station, four stops from Kita Yamagata station. Uzen Nagasaki has a rich and diverse religious tradition, and there are fourteen Buddhist temples of differing sects within walking distance of each other. These days, the temples are predominantly Sōtō-Zen and Pure Land affiliated, but near the train station you can find a large stone statue of Dainichi, housed inside an open-air wooden hut, which suggests there was once a Shingon influence in the area.

Inside Tenjōji's main hall, a Shaka triad takes the central position, surrounded on both sides by a multitude of Buddhist deities and Zen patriarchs. The statue of Ashuku is displayed in a cabinet to the left of the main display. The gold-painted statue was installed in the temple in 1992, the inauguration year of the Thirteen Buddha pilgrimage.

Heisenji(平泉寺)   Sect: Tendai   Honzon: Dainichi

Heisenji is one of four temples conveniently located in Yamagata city, about thirty minutes walk from Yamagata station. The temple is nicely situated amongst idyllic woodland on the outskirts of the city close to Chitose mountain. The *honzon* Dainichi dates from the 10th century. It is carved from wood and measures just over a meter tall. It is now housed inside a separate construct at the rear of the temple, known as the *Dainichidō*, which is dated 1684.

Dainichi is portrayed sitting cross-legged with his hands resting on his lap (the same pose he uses in the Womb World mandala). Beside him are two figures known as *Tenbu* 天部 who are dated from the late Heian era. These were originally Hindu gods *(Deva)* who were incorporated into Buddhism as protectors of the Buddhist law. They both stand triumphantly on top of cowering *Jaki* demons with their right arms raised. Wood-carved statues of Jizō and Fudō from the Edo era can also be seen in the display.

Banshōji (萬松寺)　Sect: Soto-Zen　　Honzon: Kokūzō

Banshōji is approximately a fifty-minute walk from Yamagata station. Head east along route 286 and you will find the temple located at the base of Chitose mountain. The temple is around three hundred years old and was constructed from a resilient pinewood gathered from the surrounding forest. According to ancient folklore, the pinewood is protected by the spirit of Princess Akoya (Akoya hime 阿古屋姫), who once enchanted the forest with her music.

The temple displays a Shaka triad in the main hall. Kokūzō is housed in a separate building in the outer grounds. The gold-painted statue is about 50cm tall and is placed on a table with various food offerings and incense sticks. Kokūzō sits cross-legged, holding a sword in his right hand and a wish giving pearl in his left hand.

GLOSSARY OF TERMS

Bosatsu 菩薩 Bodhisattvas.
Butsudō 仏堂 A kind of hut which houses a Buddhist monument, typically a statue or a mandala.
Gyakushū 逆修 Premortem rituals and offerings made to Buddhist deities in preparation for one's own death.
Honjibutsu 本地仏 The original Buddhist identity of a Shinto or Taoist deity.
Honji suijaku 本地垂迹 The theory that non-buddhist deities, such as Shintō Kami, are merely Buddhist deities manifesting themselves in a different form.
Honzon 本尊 The central or main deities of worship within a particular Buddhist sect.
Itabi 板碑 - Steles: blocks of stone with carved inscriptions.
Jūsainichi shinkō 十斎日信仰 The practice of worshipping ten individual Buddhist deities within a calendar month.
Nyorai 如来 Buddhas: enlightened beings.
Rokudō 六道 The six realms of existence to which beings are reincarnated.
Sanzon 三尊 The arrangement of three Buddhas to form a trinity.
Sanjūnichi hibutsu 三十日秘仏 The practice of worshipping thirty individual Buddhist deities within a calendar month.
Shominshinkō 庶民信仰 Folk religious practices and beliefs.
Shūji 種子 Sanskrit Seed syllables. They are often used to represent a Buddhist deity.
Tsuizen kuyō 追善供養 Postmortem ritual offerings to Buddhist deities for the benefit of the deceased.

NOTES AND REFERENCES

[1] The 3 Mysteries (Mudra, Mantra, Meditation) are a central component of Shingon teachings. "The practitioner identifies his own body with the body of the Buddha by making the appropriate mudra, identifies his own speech with the speech of the Buddha by reciting the appropriate mantra and identifies his own mind with the mind of the Buddha by entering into the appropriate meditative state" (Payne, 1999, p.224). By doing so, the practitioner aims to cultivate the body speech and mind of Dainichi Nyōrai that inheres within himself and all sentient beings.

[2] Gerald Massey suggested that septenaries such as the Seven Elohim of Genesis, the Seven Pitris or Fathers in India, the Seven sons of Sydik in Phoenician Mythology and the Seven sons of Ptah in Egyptian Mythology can all be traced back to the seven primordial powers of space and time. According to Massey, these septenaries were aligned with the seven constellations which turned round with the Great Bear in describing the circle of a year (See Massey, 2009).

[3] This diary covers a period of fifty-one years during the life of Fujiwara no Munetada (1062-1141).

[4] In actual fact, the ritual of holding ten feasts existed long before *The Scripture on the Ten Kings*. Teiser notes that Taoist texts show the practice may have existed as far back as the sixth century (1994, p.53).

[5] The full Japanese title for this scripture is *Bussetsu Jizō-bosatsu hosshin innen Jūō kyō* 仏説地蔵菩薩発心因縁十王経. I refer to it here in its abbreviated form: *Jizō Jūō kyō* 地蔵十王教.

[6] As the precise origin of the scripture is unknown, it still remains possible that the script is of Chinese heritage. Stephen Teiser suggests that it may have been put together as far back

as the year 1000 in a process spanning several centuries that included Chinese and Japanese versions now lost.

[7] The *Jijūhyakuinenshū* 私聚百因縁集 is a Pure Land affiliated text compiled in 1257. It lists the Ten Kings with their *honjibutsu* and most scholars agree that it postdates *The Scripture on Jizō and the Ten Kings*.

[8] *Hōbutsushū* 宝物集 compiled by Jūshin 住信 in 1179 includes one of the earliest Japanese records of the Ten Kings. However, it does not affiliate them with Buddhist deities (see Watanabe, 1989, p.166).

[9] The *Kagakushū* is a Japanese dictionary or encyclopedia dated 1444. The list of Thirteen Buddhas is kept in the same order as the *Gyakushu nikkinokoto* but the premortem date for Miroku is dated the fifth of the sixth month, instead of the fifteenth of the sixth month.

[10] Lucia Dolce suggests these Buddhas may have been the origin for a very similar tradition—the "thirty protecting deities" (*sanjūbanjin*), which used kami as protectors instead of Buddhist deities (see Teuween and Rambelli, 2003, p.226).

[11] We can also see a similar parallel with the thirty-third degree of Scottish Rite of Freemasonry which is the highest attainable degree awarded only on an honorary basis.

[12] The following website records close to two hundred *itabi* of the Amida triad found in Japan dated from the 13th to the 16th century: http://www.geocities.jp/kawai24jp/

BIBLIOGRAPHY

Abe, Ryūichi
1995   "Saichō and Kūkai A Conflict of Interpretations" *Japanese Journal of Religious Studies*, Vol 22, No.1/2. Pp.103-137.

Arai, Yūsei 新居祐政
2003   *Shingon shu Shingyō kyōten* 真言宗信行教典. Kamakura shinsho.

Cuevas, Brian J and Stone, Jaqueline I, ed.
2007   *The Buddhist Dead Practices, Discourses, Representations.* Honolulu: University of Hawai'i Press.

De Visser, M.W
1931   *The Bodhisattva Ākāsagarbha (Kokūzō) In China & Japan.* Amsterdam: Royal Dutch Academy.

Dolce Lucia and Matsumoto Ikuyo (ed.)
2010   *The Power of Ritual The World of Religious Practice in Medieval Japan* 儀礼の力中世宗教の実践世界. Kyoto: Hōzōkan

Evans-Wentz, Walter
2000   *The Tibetan Book of the Dead*. USA: OUP.

Frederic, Louis
1995   *Buddhism*. Flammarion: Paris.

Gerhart, Karen M
2009   *The Material Culture of Death in Japan.* USA: University of Hawai'i Press.

Glassman, Hank
2012   *The Face of Jizō*. Honolulu: University of Hawai'i Press.

Hakeda, Y.S.
1972   *Kūkai Major Works.* New York: Colombia University Press.

Hall, Manly.P
1967   *Buddhism and Psychotherapy.* Los Angeles: The Philosophical Research Society.

Hayami, Tasuku 速水侑
1996   *Kannon, Jizō, Fudō* 観音・地蔵・不動.
Kōdansha gendaishinsho.

Hazama Jikō
1987   "The Characteristics of Japanese Tendai" *Japanese Journal of Religious Studies*, Vol 14, No.2-3. Pp.101-112

Hori, Ichiro
1974   *Folk Religion in Japan Continuity and Change.* USA: The University of Chicago Press.

Kawakatsu, Masatarō
1969   "Jūsanbutsu shinkō no shiteki tenkai" 十三仏信仰の史的展開. *Journal of Ōtemae College*, no 03 pp.94-111 「大手前女子大学論集」第三号

Kiyota, Minoru
1978   *Shingon Buddhism.* Los Angeles: Buddhist Books International.

Komine, Kazuko 小峰和子 and Komine Michihiko 小峰彌彦
2009   *Jūsanbutsu no kanshō to egakikata* 十三仏の鑑賞と描き方. Tōkyō : Taishō Daigaku Shuppankai

Massey, Gerald
2009   Gerald Massey's Lectures. Evergreen Review, Inc.

Matsunaga Yūkei 松長有慶
2011   *Mikkyō* 密教. Tokyo : Iwanami

Miyata, Taisen
2006   *Thirteen Buddhas.* Koyasan Betsuin Temple.

Miyasaka, Yūkō 宮坂宥洪
2011 "Jūsanbutsu shinkō no igi" 十三仏信仰の意義. *Gendai Mikkyō*, no 23 現代密教第 23 号目次.

Mcarthur, Meher
2002 *Reading Buddhist Art an Illustrated Guide to Buddhist Signs & Symbols*. United Kingdom: Thames and Hudson.

Payne, Richard Karl
1991 *The Tantric Ritual of Japan Feeding the Gods: The Shingon Fire Ritual*. New Delhi: Adiya Prakashan.

Phillips, Quitman E
2003 "Narrating the Salvation of the Elite: The *Jōfukuji* Paintings of the Ten Kings". *Ars Orientalis,* Vol. 33, pp.120-145.

Saunders, Ernest Dale
1985 *Buddhism in Japan*. USA: Princeton University Press.

Sanford, Le Fleur, ed.
1992 *Flowing Traces Buddhism in the Literary and Visual Arts of Japan*. New Jersey: Princeton University Press.

Sanford, James
1997 "Wind, Waters, Stupas, Mandalas: Fetal Buddhahood in Shingon." *Japanese Journal of Religious Studies*, Vol 24, No.1/2. Pp. 1-38.

Sano, Kenji 佐野賢治
1996 *Kokūzō Bosatsu Shinkō no Kenkyū,* 虚空蔵菩薩信仰の研究. Yoshikawa Kōbunkan

Scheid, Bernhard and Teeuwen, Mark (Ed.)
2007 *The Culture of Secrecy in Japanese Religion*. London & New York: Routledge.

Sharf, Robert
1993 "The Zen of Japanese Nationalism." *History of Religions*, Vol 33, (Aug., 1993) No.1, Pp. 1-43.

Shimizu, Kunihiko 清水邦彦
2002 *"Jizō jūōkyō kō"* 「地蔵十王経」考. *Journal of Indian and Buddhist Studies*, 51 (1) pp.189-194

Snodgrass, Adrian
1988 *The Matrix and Diamond World Mandalas.* New Delhi: Adiya Prakashan.

Snodgrass, Adrian
1992 *Symbolism of the Stupa.* India: Motilal Banarsidass Publishers.

Sponberg, Alan and Hardacre Helen, ed.
1988 *Maitreya the Future Buddha.* Cambridge: Cambridge University Press.

Stone, Jaqueline I
1999 "Placing Nichiren in the Big Picture". *Japanese Journal of Religious Studies*, Vol 26, No.3/4. Pp.383-421.

Stone, Jaqueline I and Walter, Mariko Namba
2009 *Death and the Afterlife in Japanese Buddhism.* Honolulu: University of Hawai'i Press.

Taijō, Tamamuro 圭室諦成
1986 *Sōshiki Bukkyō* 葬式仏教. Daihōrinkaku.

Tanabe, George. J, ed.
1999 *Religions of Japan in Practice.* Princeton University Press.

Teeuwen, Mark and Rambelli Fabio, ed.
2003 *Buddhas and Kami in Japan Honji Suijaku as a combinatory paradigm.* London: Routledge.

Teiser, Stephen F
1994 *The Scripture on the Ten Kings and the Making of Purgatory in Medieval Chinese Buddhism.* Honolulu: University of Hawaii Press.

Teeuwen, Mark and Rambelli, Fabio
2003 *Buddhas and Kami in Japan.* London: Routledge.

Wakabayashi, Haruko
2009 "Officials of the Afterworld Ono no Takamura and the Ten Kings of Hell" *Japanese Journal of Religious Studies*, 36 (2): pp.319-342.

Watanabe, Shōgo 渡辺章悟
1989 *Tsuizenkuyō no Butsusama Jūsanbutsushinkō* 追善供養の仏さま十三仏信仰 Hokushindō.

Watarai Zuiken, et.al. 度会瑞顕
2012 *Jūsanbutsu no sekai tsuizenkuyō no rekishi shisō bunka* 十三仏の世界——追善供養の歴史・思想・文化. Nonburusha publications.

Williams, Duncan Ryūken
2005 *The Other Side of Zen.* Princeton University Press: Oxford

Yajima, Arata 矢島 新
1990 "Numatashi Shōkakujizō Jūōzu to Jyūsanbutsu Seiritsu no Mondai" 沼田市正覚寺蔵十王図と十三仏成立の問題. *Bulletin of Gunma Prefectural Women's College*, no10, pp.63-73.

Yamasaki, Taikō
1988 *Shingon Japanese Esoteric Buddhism.* Boston: Shambhala Publications Inc

十三仏

The Thirteen Buddhas
Tracing the Roots of the Thirteen Buddha Rites

Steven.J.Hutchins

www.13buddhas.com

Steven.J.Hutchins holds an MA in Japanese Studies from SOAS University of London. He has lived in Japan for over a decade.